Coding for Ki

and Up

Coding for Kids and Beginners using html,

css and JavaScript

Table of Contents

Disclaimer

Introduction

Rob had been in front of his computer for a few hours. He was in the middle of programming the next version of his JavaScript game. After making a lot of progress in the last month, he was now stuck. He tried a lot of different things, but still just cannot make it work. This is a common problem in coding. Learning the basics of coding is a good start. Rob read my first coding book (Coding for Kids Ages 9-15) a few months ago and he was very excited. Not only did learn the basics well and successfully went through all the exercises; he also implemented some of his own programs and fun coding games. He loved programming; and he was hooked.

After a couple of months, however, Rob got stuck. He was getting tired and bored. He kept doing similar programs over and over. He struggled with more advanced topics. The story of Rob is similar to those of thousands of kids across America and the world. These kids have the resources and money available to move forward. Some of their parents have spent a month's salary (sometimes even more) to get their child a laptop to program with. However, both the parents and their kids realize that they need more to get going. There is something missing. Something that is hard to quantify.

The story of Rob and others inspired me to write the next Javascript book. While Rob might seem to be struggling, he needs to be commended for his effort. Too many of us give up at the first sight of difficulty. We move on from activity to activity with the mindset of a kitten playing with a ball of yarn. The truth is that there is no movement forward in any activity without a little bit of effort and pain. Rob just needs that little bit more, and that's contained in this book.

This book starts off with some of the basics to ensure that you have the basic knowledge needed to more forward. We'll talk about setting up your workspace and doing basic programming and testing. However, this book does have a strong emphasis on coding games, activities and puzzles. These are meant to embed a deeper love for what programming can accomplish. We realize how important these kind of coding games are to the learning process. It imbibes a sense of fun and curiosity which is very exciting for everyone involved. There is also a very important section on the softer side of programming. This chapter talks about how to improve your coding through self-discovery, teamwork, self-discipline and healthy habits. These are the

soft skills that would really help Rob move forward in programming.

Soft Skills of Coding

My experiences with teaching kids coding, and also from hearing from Rob have convinced me that soft skills are just as important as technical knowledge in coding. These soft skills also help you with all other aspects of life moving forward. So, it's a win-win all the way around.

So, what exactly are soft skills? Soft skills relate more to how people work. This is different from hard technical skills which focus on what people work on. Soft skills relate to how people deal with mental, physical and interpersonal problems. In combination with good technical knowledge, soft skills can take your performance to a higher level. Here are some of the skills that I am talking about:

1. **Focus and Concentration:** Ability to focus on a single task at hand is a tough skill to master in a world dominated by social media and other distractions. Multi-tasking may seem cool; but in the long run it takes away from quality work and quality education.

a. A new tool to help you focus is something called isochronic tones. This is specific music that gets your mind in the right frame and helps you focus. You can check out these tones for free by searching 'isochronic tones' on Youtube or Google.

b. Another tool is daily meditation. Meditation for 5 minutes at the start of the day can help you build focus over time.

c. And finally, breaking your work down into periods of 20-30 minutes can make a big difference. Take a 5-10 minute walk between each session and come back refreshed.

2. **Perseverance:** The ability to persist and learn from failures is very important in coding. It's common practice among programmers to try to break the code (or make the code fail) so they can learn the weak points in a program, and make it improve. You can do the same for your program and for your programming skill.

3. **Teamwork:** Going at coding alone is necessary when starting off; but will hold you back in the long run. You can learn a lot faster from the mistakes of others; than from your own mistakes. You can join a local programming club in your own city; hire a programming tutor; join relevant facebook coding groups; post on redditt threads and learn

from Github code. It's important to be active on these groups and recognized as a positive contributor.

4. **Physical Health:** This is a very underrated and undervalued trait by many programmers. But in the long run, it really hurts people in the industry. Back problems, obesity, carpal tunnel syndrome are common health issues that programmers encounter after working in the industry for 5-10 years or more. Here's a few ways to take better care of your health.

   a. Maintain a good sitting posture: Sit upright. Make sure your laptop is close to eye level, so you don't have to bend your neck down. Make sure your feet are in line with your knees.

   b. Take frequent breaks: I recommend taking breaks every 20-30 minutes. Take a walk in between periods.

   c. Diet: Maintain a healthy diet high in good fats, protein and complex carbs. Minimize simple carbs and sugar.

   d. Exercise: Maintain a regular exercise regime or play a sport. It's important to exercise at least 3-4 times a week (maybe more).

e. Sleep: Get at least 7-8 hours of sleep every night. If you're unable to sleep, ask a qualified doctor how you can improve your sleep.

One can write entire books on each of the above topics; but this is a coding book, so I will leave it there. Just remember that the above soft skills are very important and you can work on them while you are coding as well.

Setting Up Your Workspace

What You Need

You need a laptop/desktop with an internet connection, and a web browser installed. I recommend using Mozilla Firefox or Google Chrome.

Download/Install Text Editing software

Download the latest version of a text editing software. I recommend downloading NotePad++. Once you download, double click the Setup.exe file and follow the installation prompts.

https://notepad-plus-plus.org/downloads/

Open Notepad++ from your Desktop or Start Menu

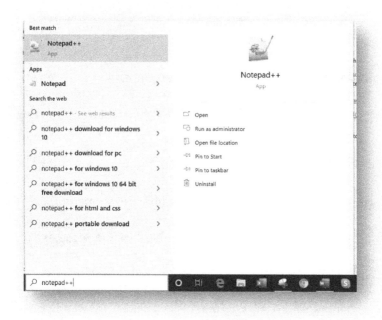

Now, click **File>New** to open a New File.

21

Now, choose **File>Save** As and choose **.html** as the file type

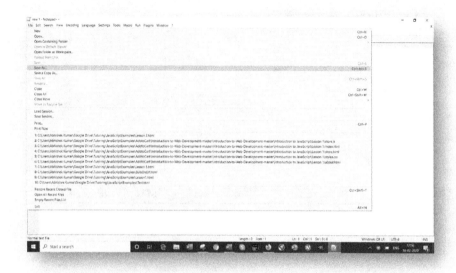

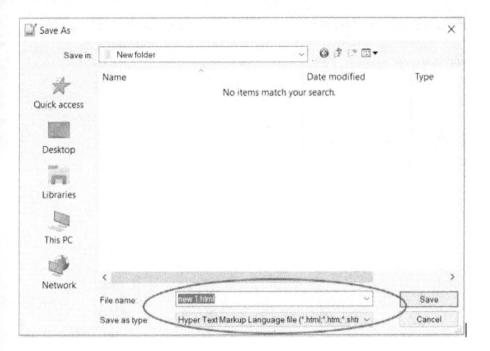

Test Program

Now, let's test if the program connects with the browser.

Just type in random text in your file. In my file, I've typed **"This is a Test Message."**

Now **File>Save**.

After that, click **Run>Launch in Firefox/Chrome/IE** depending on which browser you are using.

If it is working, the text that you typed in should show in the browser window.

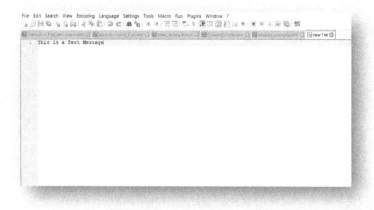

tml - Notepad++

Run Plugins Window ?

Run...	F5
Launch in Firefox	Ctrl+Alt+Shift+X
Launch in IE	Ctrl+Alt+Shift+I
Launch in Chrome	Ctrl+Alt+Shift+R
Launch in Safari	Ctrl+Alt+Shift+A
Get PHP help	Alt+F1
Wikipedia Search	Alt+F3
Open file in another instance	Alt+F6
Send via Outlook	Ctrl+Alt+Shift+O
Modify Shortcut/Delete Command...	

Result:

This is a Test Message

This is a great simple way to ensure that your program is working before

moving forward.

Aside:

One issue that some students have encountered is that the run browser option sometimes does not work and gives an error. This is because the path is not set right. If, for some reason, it doesn't work, you can still run the program.

1. Just save the Notepad++ as a html document.

2. Close the Notepad++ file.

3. Go the folder where the html document is.

4. Double click on the html file and it should work.

What is html?

html stands for Hyper Text Markup Language.

It is the programming language that we use to interact with the internet

through web pages. The basic structure of all web pages is defined by html.

It is simple enough for beginner programmers to grasp quickly.

Most html programming is done by items called tags. These tags start with <>

And end with </>. For example, a common tag is the paragraph tag which

begins with <p> and ends with </p>.

Common html Tags

<html> - This tag is used at the start of every webpage to denote the start of

html code

<head> - This piece of html code is executed before the rest of the program

<title> - This tag is used the title the web page. It writes the text on to the top ribbon of the webpage.

<body> - This is the information on the body of the web page.

<h1> - Used to denote a heading tag. This is the largest size heading tag.

<h2>,<h3>,<h4>,<h5>,<h6> - Used to denote subheadings of decreasing size.

<p> - Used to denote paragraphs of text

<img> - This shows an image on the web page. This image either links to an external web page or to an internal file.

<strong> - Added to make text bold

<ul> - This is for an unordered list. An example of this would be a list of items in bullet form.

<li> - Adds a bullet item to an unordered list.

<ol> - This is for ordered lists such as numbered lists from 1,2,3....

<div> - Used to denote larger sections of text; that contain several paragraphs..

<a> - Used to link items in a web page to another web page.

**
** - Adds a line break to the code and moves to the next line.

Example of html code

Below is an example of basic html code. It has examples of all the above html codes. You can type these out or copy paste the example below that.

```
1   <html>
2   <head>
3   <title>My first html website......</title>
4   </head>
5   <body>
6   <h1>Welcome to Programming in Javascript (this is a h1 tag)</h1>
7   <h2>Let's get started (this is a h2 tag)</h2>
8   <h3>This is the start of bigger things (this is a h3 tag)</h3>
9   <p>We're going over a few basic html tags here but you can feel free to play around them and experiment.
10  There are 1000's of html tags that you can learn in the long run. Here's a list of topics you can learn below (This is a paragraph tag)</p>
11
12  <ul> Below is the example of an unordered bulleted list
13  <li>Basics of html</li>
14  <li>CSS</li>
15  <li>JavaScript</li>
16  <li>Loops</li>
17  <li>Arrays</li>
18  <li>Canvas</li>
19  </ul>
20
21  <a href="https://www.google.com">Example of hyperlink to Google</a><br>
22  <a href="https://www.facebook.com">Example of hyperlink to Facebook</a><br>
23  <a href="https://www.amazon.com">Example of hyperlink to Amazon</a><br>
24
25  </body>
26  </html>
27  ]
```

Copy Paste Version of html code

You can copy and paste below code into your html browser to see if it works

<html>

<head>

<title>My first html website......</title>

</head>

<body>

<h1>Welcome to Programming in Javascript (this is a h1 tag)</h1>

<h2>Let's get started (this is a h2 tag)</h2>

<h3>This is the start of bigger things (this is a h3 tag)</h3>

<p>We're going over a few basic html tags here but you can feel free to play around them and experiment.

There are 1000's of html tags that you can learn in the long run. Here's a list of topics you can learn below (This is a paragraph tag)</p>

<ul> Below is the example of an unordered bulleted list

<li>Basics of html</li>

<li>CSS</li>

<li>JavaScript</li>

<li>Loops</li>

<li>Arrays</li>

<li>Canvas</li>

```html
</ul>

<a href="https://www.google.com">Example of hyperlink to Google</a><br>

<a href="https://www.facebook.com">Example of hyperlink to

Facebook</a><br>

<a href="https://www.amazon.com">Example of hyperlink to

Amazon</a><br>

</body>

</html>
```

Code Output

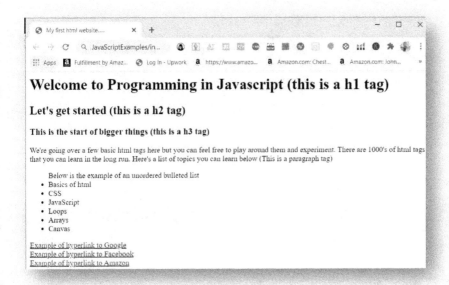

Now, let's break down the different elements:

Below is the title tag <title>

Below are the heading tags <h1>,<h2>,<h3>

Welcome to Programming in Javascript (this is a h1 tag)

Let's get started (this is a h2 tag)

This is the start of bigger things (this is a h3 tag)

Below is the paragraph tag `<p>`

We're going over a few basic html tags here but you can feel free to play around them and experiment. There are 1000's of html tags that you can learn in the long run. Here's a list of topics you can learn below (This is a paragraph tag)

Below is an unordered bulleted list `<ul>` `<li>`

- Basics of html
- CSS
- JavaScript
- Loops
- Arrays
- Canvas

Below are 3 hyperlink tags to 3 popular websites `<a href>`

Example of hyperlink to Google
Example of hyperlink to Facebook
Example of hyperlink to Amazon

Practice Problems

1. Make a website with a title tag that has a list of grocery items in an unordered list. Use a paragraph tag to indicate any special instructions you may have for particular items. At the end of the list, use a hyperlink tag to link to the website of the closest grocery store.

2. Create a website with a list of all the players on your soccer team. Use a title, heading and paragraph tag to welcome users to your website and describe the team and the philosophy of the team. Use an ordered list to list the players.

3. Make a website that lists all your favorite restaurants and coffee shops in your area in an unordered list. Use a title, heading and paragraph tag to introduce yourself and the dining experience in your area.

Sample html Program

What This Project Does

This html project creates two buttons. These two buttons switch between two images of Day and Night. The two buttons are labelled 'Day' and 'Night'

This is a simple html project that creates a button that can switch a light bulb on the page on/off. We are going to use two bulb images to make this happen. The button will switch between the two images.

Concepts to Understand for this Chapter

We'll need to understand button tags and image tags for this example.

Button Tag

<button onclick=Action >Button text</button>

The button element has two elements. An Action and Button Text. The Button Text is the text that shows on the button; and the Action is what happens when the user clicks on the button

Image Tag

<img id=ImageId src=ImageUrl style=ImageSize>

The Image Tag has three elements.

The **ImageId** is the name you assign to the image. This name is used to reference the image in the code.

Imageurl is the url of the image that the tag is referencing. If the image is in the same folder as the html file, then you can use the file name only instead of the entire url.

ImageSize sets the width and height of the Image. The width and height are in pixels.

Files

Here are the two files that you need to use for the next project. You can download these and save it in the same folder that you are going to create the html file.

Day Picture

Night Picture

Code

```
j<html>
j<body>

<h2>Day and Night Buttons</h2>

<button onclick="document.getElementById('myImage').src='DayImage.jpg'">Day</button>

<img id="myImage" src="DayImage.jpg" style="width:200px">

<button onclick="document.getElementById('myImage').src='NightImage.jpg'">Night</button>

</body>
</html>
```

Output

Initially, the default is set to Day Image.

Day and Night Buttons

Once, you click the **Night** button, you get:

Day and Night Buttons

Day   Night

Then, when you click **Day** button again, you get:

Day and Night Buttons

Day   Night

40

Code Explained

```
<img id="myImage" src="DayImage.jpg" style="width:200px">
```

The above html element is an image tag. It has 3 elements; id, src and style.

id is a label for the image. In this case, it is labelled as "myImage". The id is used to reference the image throughout the program.

src is the source of the image the tag loads. The image "DayImage.jpg" is in the same folder as the html file.

```
<button onclick="document.getElementById('myImage').src='DayImage.jpg'">Day</button>
```

The above element is a button element. It has a parameter called **onclick** which describes what action is done when clicking the button.

document.getElementById obtains the element with id 'myImage'. So it displays 'DayImage.jpg' on 'myImage' when you click the button.

'Day' is the text written on the button.

```
<buttononclick="document.getElementById('myImage').src='NightImage.jpg'>Night</button>
```

document.getElementById obtains the element with id 'myImage'. So, it displays 'NightImage.jpg' on 'MyImage' when the button is clicked.

'Night' is the text written on the button.

Practice Problems

1. Find 3 images of a person running, walking and standing still. Write a program with 3 buttons where the person runs, walks or stands till based on the button your press.

2. Find 3 images of a traffic light with red, green and orange light on. Write a program with 3 buttons that say 'STOP', 'GO' and 'WATCH'. The traffic light switches to red when 'STOP' button is pressed; switches to green when 'GO' button is pressed; and to yellow when 'WATCH' button is pressed.

html forms

Remember those forms you see online where you enter your name and age and date of birth? Those are html forms.

Today, we're going to learn how to make those.

Before we start making forms, we need to learn about a few basic form elements:

Button <button> - It is an element that allows the user to perform an action when clicked.

Textbox <input> - This element allows the user to type text into a box on the browser screen. It's used to collect small text items like name, city etc.

Textarea <textarea> - This allows the user to input larger quantities of text. It is bigger in size than the textbox. It's used for larger text items like address, comments etc.

Option Select<select> - This element allows the user to select between several available options. It's basically a drop-down box.

Date Input<input type="date"> - This elements allows the user to choose a

date from a calendar drop down.

Now, let's go through each of these examples through a sample form below.

Sample Form

```
<html>
  <head><title>Sample Form</title></head>
  <body>
  <form id="form1">
    Enter First Name:<input name="frstname" type="text" id="frstname" size="20"><br>
    Enter Last Name:<input name="lname" type="text" id="lname" size="20"><br><br>
    Enter Address: <textarea name="TextBox" cols="40" rows="5" id="tstr2"></textarea><br><br>
    Enter Country: <select id="country" name="country">
                     <option value="USA">USA</option>
                     <option value="Mexico">Mexico</option>
                     <option value="Canada">Canada</option>
                     <option value="Australia">Australia</option>
                   </select><br>
    Date of Birth: <input type="date" id="start" name="trip-start"
                   value="2020-07-22"
                   min="1918-01-01" max="2020-06-31"><br>
    <button onclick="">Submit</button>

  </body>
  </html>
```

Now, let's go through each part of the code.

```
<form id="form1">
```

Each form starts with the <form> html element. The id **"form1"** is the name

that you give the form. The id is used to reference the form in the rest of the

program.

```
Enter First Name:<input name="frstname" type="text" id="frstname" size="20"><br>
Enter Last Name:<input name="lname" type="text" id="lname" size="20"><br><br>
```

44

The above 2 lines are textboxes for first and last name. The type is assigned to **"text"** because name is a form of text. The id **"frstname"** and **"lname"** will be used to reference the code if we need to later. The size is set to **"20"** which means it can accept 20 characters. You can change it to a larger or shorter size as needed.

```
Enter Address: <textarea name="TextBox" cols="40" rows="5" id="tstr2"></textarea><br><br>
```

The above element is a textarea element for the address. It has 5 rows (rows="5") and 40 characters per row (cols="40"). It is labelled as "tstr2".

```
Enter Country: <select id="country" name="country">
               <option value="USA">USA</option>
               <option value="Mexico">Mexico</option>
               <option value="Canada">Canada</option>
               <option value="Australia">Australia</option>
               </select><br>
```

The above element is a select option element for choosing a country. It allows you to select between a drop-down menu of 4 different options; USA, Mexico, Canada and Australia. It is labelled as "country" **(id="country")**.

```
Date of Birth: <input type="date" id="start" name="trip-start"
               value="2020-07-22"
               min="1918-01-01" max="2020-06-31"><br>
```

The above element is an input date element, that lets you choose a date of birth between 1918 (**min="1918-01-01"**) and 2020(**max="2020-06-31"**). It is named as "start" (**id="start"**) and is set to a value of 2020-07-22 (**value="2020-07-22"**).

```
<button onclick="">Submit</button>
```

The above element is a button element. It has the text "Submit" written on it. It does nothing on clicking as the onclick function is empty.

Now, let's have a look at what happens when we run the program.

Output:

Enter First Name: [   ]
Enter Last Name: [   ]

Enter Address: [   ]

Enter Country: [USA ⌄]
Date of Birth: [22 / 07 / 2020 ⊗]
[Submit]

I hope you learned a bit about the basics of html forms with this example. In the next few chapters, we'll learn how to use the information we input using

JavaScript. In fact, we'll use this same example and print it out using JavaScript.

Practice Problems

1. Write a html form that is a resume for a university student. It accepts first name, last name, university name through a textbox; university year through a drop down. Then there are 3 activities/internships/co-ops. Each activity has a from date element, to date element and a textarea large enough to describe the experience. End with a submit button.

2. Write a html form for a grocery list. It accepts first name, last name, date of shopping, address and city. It has 5 drop down with 30 common grocery items to choose form. And finally, it has a submit button.

Each of the above will be expanded on with JavaScript in the coming chapter.

What is JavaScript?

JavaScript is a high-level programming language that is used to make web pages more interactive and dynamic. It is text-based and user-friendly.

While html is used to create a web page structure and css is for web page style, JavaScript is used to make the web page more interactive with the user. It allows different html elements to interact with each other, performs calculations, animations etc. In other words, it makes web page programming fun.

Using JavaScript with html

There are two ways to use JavaScript in a html web page. The first way is to just add the code within script tags in html. This is shown in the blue portion of the code below.

```
<html>

<head><title>Test file 1</title>

</head>
```

```
<body>

<script>

//Enter JavaScript code here

</script>

</body>

</html>
```

The 2nd way is to create an external JavaScript file that contains the code and save it as a .js file. Then you can link the file to the html content. For example, let's say you create a file called 'test.js'. You can link it using the blue portion of the code below:

```
<html>

<head><title>Test file 2</title>

</head>
```

```
<body>

<script src=" test.js"></script>

</body>

</html>
```

JavaScript Elements

With that basic knowledge, let's have a look at some basic JavaScript elements.

functions

A function in JavaScript is a set of lines of code that performs a certain task.

It is defined in JavaScript within the script tags as:

```
function afunc()

{

//Enter function code here

}
```

The name of the function is afunc and the code within the curly brackets is executed each time afunc is called on.

It is useful to have functions when we want to perform the same task several times in the same program. We can just call on the function instead of writing the same lines of code several times.

Variables

A variable in JavaScript is a placeholder that takes on a certain value. The value can be changed throughout the program and can be used in other parts of the code. Let's take an example:

```
var x=5;
```

x is the variable defined. It starts with a value of 5.

Later on, in the program, it can be changed to a different value, as in:

```
x=10;
```

Now, x has a value of 10. And, if we do:

```
x=x-1;
```

Then x becomes 9. What we just showed is an integer variable. We can also

have string variables used to store text values, as in:

var b="abcd"

b is a variable that holds the value abcd.

And finally, we can have Boolean variables that holds only true/false values.

For example:

var c = true;

var d = (7>5);

var e = (7<6);

Variables c,d and e are all Boolean variables. Variable c is assigned to true.

Variable d is true (because 7 is greater than 5). Variable e is false (because 7

is not less than 6).

document.write()

document.write() is used to print elements on the web page. Anything that is within the brackets is printed on the web page. For example:

```
document.write("Example print");
```

The above line prints the words **"Example print"** on the screen.

We can also print variables on the screen. For example,

```
var a=7;
```

```
document.write(a)
```

Above line prints 7 on the screen.

And, we can combine different elements also using "+" operator. For example:

```
var a=7;
```

```
document.write("The number printed is "+a);
```

The above line prints "The number printed is 7".

alert()

Alert puts a pop-up on the screen with a particular message. For example,

alert("Hello")

The above message has a pop-up message that says "Hello"

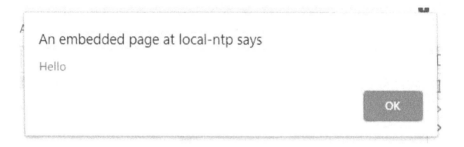

An embedded page at local-ntp says

Hello

OK

prompt()

prompt has the same popup but what a textbox that allows user input. The user input can be stored in a variable. For example:

var name = prompt("What is your name");

It shows a pop-up. Once the user enters his name and says ok, it stores the value in the variable name.

An embedded page at local-ntp says

What is your name

|

OK   Cancel

document.getElementById().value

Document.getElementById().value is used to get html elements into JavaScript variables. So, we need to use the id of the html element and put it in between brackets. Let's look at an example.

Let's look at below html element:

Enter number: <input name="x" type="number" id="test" size="20">

JavaScript code:

```
var testv=document.getElementById("test").value;
```

The html element is a form textbox that accepts a number from the user.

In Javascript, the number that the user assigns is set to the variable testv.

How to add Comments

Comments are items that you add to the code to document or explain the code. Comments cannot be executed and do not effect the program.

Comments in JavaScript are added using two double backslash in front of the comment ("//")

```html
<html>
<head>
<title>Print Name and Age......</title>
</head>
<body>
<form id="form1">
Enter Name: <input name="Enter Name" type="text" id="name" size="20"><br>
Enter Favorite Hobby: <input type="text" id="hobby" size="20"><br>
Enter Age: <input type="number" id="age" size="20"><br>
</form>
<button onclick="writename()">Print Intro</button>

<script>

function writename()
{
    //Creating variables
    var nameValue=document.getElementById("name").value;
    var hobby=document.getElementById("hobby").value;
    var age=document.getElementById("age").value;

    //Prints name on screen
    document.write("This is "+nameValue+". I am "+ age+" years old.My favorite hobby is "+hobby);

}

</script>
</body>
</html>
```

Below is an example of comments. The comments are in green and circled in red.

Example 1

Now, let's start looking at some examples. We'll start with the html form in the previous chapter. We're going to assign all the user inputs into variables and print them on the web browser using JavaScript.

The code below is the similar to the example in the previous chapter.

A JavaScript function has been added to print the first name and country of the person who submitted the form.

```html
<html>
<head><title>Sample Form</title></head>
<body>
<form id="form1">
Enter First Name:<input name="frstname" type="text" id="frstname" size="20"><br>
Enter Last Name:<input name="lname" type="text" id="lname" size="20"><br><br>
Enter Address: <textarea name="TextBox" cols="40" rows="5" id="tstr2"></textarea><br><br>
Enter Country: <select id="country" name="country">
                <option value="USA">USA</option>
                <option value="Mexico">Mexico</option>
                <option value="Canada">Canada</option>
                <option value="Australia">Australia</option>
                <option value="India">Australia</option>
                </select><br>
Date of Birth: <input type="date" id="dbirth" name="trip-start"
                value="2020-07-22"
                min="1918-01-01" max="2020-06-31"><br>
<button onclick="printcountry()">Submit</button>

<script>
function printcountry()
{
var fname = document.getElementById("frstname").value;
var lname = document.getElementById("lname").value;
var address = document.getElementById("tstr2").value;
var country = document.getElementById("country").value;
var dob = document.getElementById("dbirth").value;
document.write (fname+" lives in "+country);
}
</script>


</body>
</html>
```

Output:

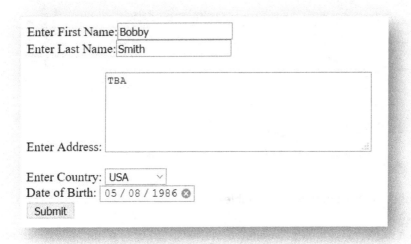

After clicking **submit**, we get:

Bobby lives in USA

The Code Explained

So the main part that we added was the function printcountry(). We also

added the function to the onclick element of the button.

(onclick="printcountry()").

```
<button onclick="printcountry()">Submit</button>
<script>
function printcountry()
{
var fname = document.getElementById("frstname").value;
var lname = document.getElementById("lname").value;
var address = document.getElementById("tstr2").value;
var country = document.getElementById("country").value;
var dob = document.getElementById("dbirth").value;
document.write (fname+" lives in "+country);
}
</script>

</body>
</html>
```

In this function, we declare five variables fname, lname, address, country, dob. Each of these variables is assigned to the values of first name, last name, address, country and dob entered in the form respectively. This is done using the document.getElementById().value JavaScript element.

Finally, we use document.write() to print out first name and dob entered in the form.

Example 2

In the second example, we create a simple JavaScript function that takes in 3 numbers and multiplies them together.

Output:

```html
<html>
<head><title>Sample Form</title></head>
<body>
<form id="form1">
Enter First Number:<input name="number1" type="number" id="num1" size="20"><br>
Enter Second Number:<input name="number2" type="number" id="num2" size="20"><br><br>
Enter Third Number: <input name="number3" type="number" id="num3" size="20"></textarea><br><br>

<button onclick="multiplynum()">Submit</button>

<script>
function multiplynum()
{
var n1 = document.getElementById("num1").value;
var n2 = document.getElementById("num2").value;
var n3 = document.getElementById("num3").value;
document.write("The product of the three numbers is "+n1*n2*n3);
}
</script>

</body>
</html>
```

Once we click, submit we get:

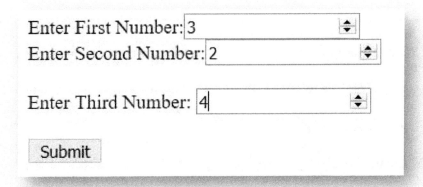

Code Explained:

In the above code, we take in three numbers in the form with id's of num1, num2 and num3.

The button runs the **multiplynum()**Javascript function when it is clicked.

In the function three variables of n1,n2,n3 are assigned to the 3 numbers in the form with id's of num1, num2 and num3 respectively.

Finally, we print out the product of the three numbers n1*n2*n3 using document.write() in the final line.

Practice Problems

1. Create the form in practice problem 1 of the previous chapter. Print out all the information in the form like a proper resume on the web page. Feel free to print it out and hand it over to an employer if it looks good enough ☺.

2. Create the form in practice problem 2 of the previous chapter. Print out the entire grocery list on the html web page. Then you can print it out on a sheet of paper and go shopping.

3. Create a form that takes in two numbers. It has 4 buttons with button text of Add, Subtract, Multiply and Divide. Each of these 4 buttons executes 4 different functions that adds, subtracts, multiplies and divides the two numbers and prints out the result.

Introduction to CSS

What is CSS?

CSS is an acronym for Cascading Style Sheets. It allows the user to set and modify the style of your html website. 'Style' is a term used for font type, font color, background color, shading etc. CSS elements can be accessed through html and JavaScript.

Create CSS file and link to html file

There are 5 steps to create a CSS file and link it to a html document.

1. To create a css file, open a black html document and save as 'CSS' file type. In this case, we're going to name it 'samplestyle'.

```
Normal text file (*.txt)
Flash ActionScript file (*.as;*.mx)
Ada file (*.ada;*.ads;*.adb)
Assembly language source file (*.asm)
Abstract Syntax Notation One file (*.mib)
Active Server Pages script file (*.asp;*.asp)
AutoIt (*.au3)
AviSynth scripts files (*.avs;*.avsi)
BaanC File (*.bc;*.cln)
Unix script file (*.bash;*.sh;*.bsh;*.csh;*.bash_profile;*.bashrc;*.profile)
Batch file (*.bat;*.cmd;*.nt)
BlitzBasic file (*.bb)
C source file (*.c;*.lex)
Categorical Abstract Machine Language (*.ml;*.mli;*.sml;*.thy)
CMake file (*.cmake;*.cmake)
COmmon Business Oriented Language (*.cbl;*.cbd;*.cdb;*.cdc;*.cob)
Csound file (*.orc;*.sco;*.csd)
CoffeeScript file (*.coffee;*.litcoffee)
C++ source file (*.h;*.hpp;*.hxx;*.cpp;*.cxx;*.cc;*.ino)
C# source file (*.cs)
Cascade Style Sheets File (*.css)
D programming language (*.d)
Diff file (*.diff;*.patch)
Erlang file (*.erl;*.hrl)
ESCRIPT file (*.src;*.em)
Forth file (*.forth)
Fortran free form source file (*.f;*.for;*.f90;*.f95;*.f2k;*.f23)
Fortran fixed form source file (*.f77)
FreeBasic file (*.bas;*.bi)
Haskell (*.hs;*.lhs;*.las)
```

shapes example	02.07.2020 19:52	Firefox HTML

File name:	samplestyple	Save
Save as type:	Cascade Style Sheets File (*.css)	Cancel

2. Go to the relevant html and include the line below in the header file.

You can do so with the line below.

```html
<html>
<head><title>Sample Form</title></head>
<body>
<link rel="stylesheet" href="samplestyle.css" />
<form id="form1">
Enter First Number:<input name="number1" type="number" id="num1" size="20"><br>
Enter Second Number:<input name="number2" type="number" id="num2" size="20"><br><br>
Enter Third Number: <input name="number3" type="number" id="num3" size="20"></textarea><br><br>

<button onclick="multiplynum()">Submit</button>

<script>
function multiplynum()
{
var n1 = document.getElementById("num1").value;
var n2 = document.getElementById("num2").value;
var n3 = document.getElementById("num3").value;
document.write("The product of the three numbers is "+n1*n2*n3);
}
</script>

</body>
</html>
```

3. (Optional) To make your button editable in css add the text class="btn" to

the html button line as shown below:

<button class = "btn submit" onclick="multiplynum()">Submit</button>

Now, Let's insert the style sheet in the example from last chapter.

```
<html>
 <head><title>Sample Form</title></head>
<body>
 <link rel="stylesheet" href="samplestyle.css" />
<form id="form1">
 Enter First Number:<input name="number1" type="number" id="num1" size="20"><br>
 Enter Second Number:<input name="number2" type="number" id="num2" size="20"><br><br>
 Enter Third Number: <input name="number3" type="number" id="num3" size="20"></textarea><br><br>

 <button class = "btn submit" onclick="multiplynum()">Submit</button>

<script>
 function multiplynum()
{
 var n1 = document.getElementById("num1").value;
 var n2 = document.getElementById("num2").value;
 var n3 = document.getElementById("num3").value;
 document.write("The product of the three numbers is "+n1*n2*n3);
 }
</script>

</body>
</html>
```

Great. Now our CSS sheet is linked to our html file.

CSS Terms

html{}, body{}: The code within the html brackets defines the styling for the entire html files. The body code within the brackets is the code for the body of the html file.

text-decoration: Can modify the text design by making it wavy, dotted, curly etc.

text-transform: Can capitalize parts or the whole text

text-align: Can align the text at the center, right or left

margin: Margin is the space between elements. It is expressed in terms of pixels. For example, margin: 5px specifies a margin of 5 pixels.

padding: Padding is the space within an element from the outer boundary. It is specified in pixels as well.

display: Can be used to completely turn off an element. (e.g. display: none switches off the element completely)

hidden: Can he used to hide an element while it still takes up space in the layout.

font-size: Specifies the size of the font.

background-color: Specifies the background color of the element. Any of the wide variety of colors in the link below can be chosen.

https://www.quackit.com/css/css_color_codes.cfm

color: Specifies the color of the written text.

border: Specifies the presence and type/style of border around an element. There can be a hidden, dotted, double border; or there can also be no border.

font-weight: Specifies the boldness of a font.

min-height: Specifies the minimum height of an element. Height is in pixels.

line-height: Specifies the height of a line of text. Height is in pixels.

.btn{} – This specifies the styling for any buttons defined in html. To make a button accessible in css, we have to include the class name in the html definition as we did in the previous example.

.btn:hover{} – Did you know that you can specify the style of a button when the mouse hovers over it? Cool, isn't it? All items within the brackets can specify the style of the button and text within the button.

To get a look at the 1000's of CSS properties out there to style your web-page look at the link below:

https://www.htmlhelp.com/reference/css/properties.html

CSS Example

```css
html, body {
    text-decoration: none;
    text-transform: capitalize;
    text-align: center;
    margin: 10;
    padding-top: 50px;
    min-height: 80%;
    color: white;
    background-color: blue;
    line-height: 1.5;
    font-family:serif;
    font-size: 25px;
    font-weight: normal;

}
.btn {
    background-color: black;
    border: none;
    color: white;
    padding: 10px 24px;
    text-align: center;
    text-decoration: none;
    display: inline-block;
    font-size: 16px;
}
.btn:hover {
    background-color: Crimson;
    color: black;
}
```

Code Explained

We first define the html and body of the code. The text is capitalized and set to the center. It is white in color against a blue background. It is 50 pixels from the top of the margin. It is normal un-bolded sans-serif font of 25 px.

The button style is defined with .btn{}. The button has white text with a black background. The text font is 16 px and is aligned to the center of the button. The style changes when we hover the mouse over the button. It changes to black text with a Crimson red background.

The css file is linked to one of our sample forms in the previous chapter. We show you the output before and after linking the css file. We see what a difference a CSS styling makes. It's like a makeover 😊

Output (Without CSS):

Enter First Number:
Enter Second Number:

Enter Third Number:

Submit

Output (with CSS):

Output (with CSS and mouse hovering over button):

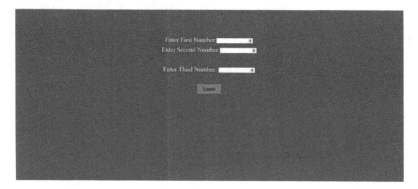

CSS And JavaScript

If a html form is linked to CSS, and JavaScript starts printing text on the web page, you notice that it is no longer linked to CSS.

What you need to do is relink the CSS in the JavaScript code using the line below:

document.write('<link rel="stylesheet" type="text/css" href="samplestyle.css" />');

Enter this code right before the start of every function in JavaScript. This ensures that css is shown for the entire program. See the example in the text below:

```
<html>
  <head><title>Sample Form</title></head>
<body>
  <link rel="stylesheet" type="text/css" href="samplestyle.css" />
<form id="form1">
  Enter First Number:<input name="number1" type="number" id="num1" size="20"><br>
  Enter Second Number:<input name="number2" type="number" id="num2" size="20"><br><br>
  Enter Third Number: <input name="number3" type="number" id="num3" size="20"></textarea><br><br>

  <button class = "btn submit" onclick="multiplynum()">Submit</button>

<script>
  function multiplynum()
{
  var n1 = document.getElementById("num1").value;
  var n2 = document.getElementById("num2").value;
  var n3 = document.getElementById("num3").value;
  document.write('<link rel="stylesheet" type="text/css" href="samplestyle.css" />');
  document.write("The product of the three numbers is "+n1*n2*n3);
}
</script>

</body>
</html>
```

Output (before adding CSS line to JavaScript):

On clicking **Submit** button:

The product of the three numbers is 60

Output (after adding CSS line to JavaScript):

On clicking **Submit** button:

1. Create a css stylesheet that specifies a style for all form elements and buttons. Link it all the previous practice problems and marvel at your creation.

2. Create a html form with 2 buttons. Create two css sheets. The 2 html buttons switch between the two stylesheets.

Doing Math with JavaScript

JavaScript is a great programming language to perform calculations and analyse data from users. We'll go over a few functions that help get you going with JavaScript.

Now, this section is not for everyone. It's only for those who are interested in implementing a lot of math in their programs, or like math and would like to see it implemented in JavaScript.

ParseInt/ParseFloat

parseInt – ParseInt takes in a string variable and returns an integer. It also takes in decimal numbers and converts them to integers.

ParseFloat – ParseFloat is similar to parseInt but works with decimal numbers.

Let's look at an example below.

In the example, we put 3 of the numbers through parseInt and the same

numbers through parseFloat. And we see the outputs.

```
<html>
 <head><title>Sample Form</title></head>
<body>
<form id="form1">

<button onclick="multiplynum()">Parse Integers</button>

<script>
 function multiplynum()
{
 xi=parseInt("5.2");
 yi=parseInt(5.01);
 zi=parseInt(5.65);
 xf=parseFloat("5.2");
 yf=parseFloat(5.01);
 zf=parseFloat(5.65);
 document.write("xi= "+xi+"<br>");
 document.write("yi= "+yi+"<br>");
 document.write("zi= "+zi+"<br>");
 document.write("xf= "+xf+"<br>");
 document.write("yf= "+yf+"<br>");
 document.write("zf= "+zf+"<br>");
}
</script>


</body>
</html>
```

Output:

xi= 5
yi= 5
zi= 5
xf= 5.2
yf= 5.01
zf= 5.65

We can see that the results are different for parseInt and parseFloat. For xi

and yi, we pass the string "5.2". It is considered a string because it is within

quotes. Even though there is a number within the quotes, we cannot use it in

any mathematical operations without actually doing a parseInt or parseFloat.

After completing a parseInt or parseFloat, it becomes a number.

We also note that for all the values parseInt removes the decimal points and

makes it a whole number. It does not round up or round down, just removes

the decimal.

ParseFloat retains the decimal value. So, if you want to work with decimals;

use ParseFloat. If you want no decimal, then use ParseInt.

Next, let's talk about rounding numbers. We use the functions **Math.Ceil()**, **Math.Floor()** and **Math.Round()**. Math.Ceil() rounds to the upper decimal value, Math.Floor() to the upper decimal value and Math.Round() to the nearest value (whether it's upper or lower). Let's look at a sample program.

```html
<html>
<head><title>Sample Form</title></head>
<body>
<form id="form1">

<button onclick="multiplynum()">Round numbers</button>

<script>
function multiplynum()
{
xc=Math.ceil(5.2);
yc=Math.ceil(7.8);
zc=Math.ceil(4.5);
xf=Math.floor(5.2);
yf=Math.floor(7.8);
zf=Math.floor(4.5);
xr=Math.round(5.2);
yr=Math.round(7.8);
zr=Math.round(4.5);
document.write("Example of Math.ceil<br>");
document.write("xc= "+xc+"<br>");
document.write("yc= "+yc+"<br>");
document.write("zc= "+zc+"<br>");
document.write("Example of Math.floor<br>");
document.write("xf= "+xf+"<br>");
document.write("yf= "+yf+"<br>");
document.write("zf= "+zf+"<br>");
document.write("Example of Math.round<br>");
document.write("xr= "+xr+"<br>");
document.write("yr= "+yr+"<br>");
document.write("zr= "+zr+"<br>");
}
</script>

</body>
</html>
```

In the code, we put 3 decimal numbers through Math.floor(), Math.ceil() and

Math.round() and the output demonstrates how the functions work.

Output:

```
Example of Math.ceil
xc= 6
yc= 8
zc= 5
Example of Math.floor
xf= 5
yf= 7
zf= 4
Example of Math.round
xr= 5
yr= 8
zr= 5
```

Add, subtract, multiply, divide

It might seem self-explanatory, but because of how vital it is to do any basic

calculation, I have to go over the 4 basic mathematical operations.

```html
<html>
<head><title>Sample Form</title></head>
<body>
<form id="form1">
Enter First Number:<input name="number1" type="number" id="num1" size="20"><br>
Enter Second Number:<input name="number2" type="number" id="num2" size="20"><br><br>

<button onclick="test()">Calculate</button>

<script>
function test()
{
var n1 = parseInt(document.getElementById("num1").value);
var n2 = parseInt(document.getElementById("num2").value);
var sum=n1+n2;
var difference=n1-n2;
var product=n1*n2;
var quotient=n1/n2;

document.write("The sum is "+sum+"<br>");
document.write("The difference is "+difference+"<br>");
document.write("The product is "+product+"<br>");
document.write("The quotient is "+quotient);

}
</script>

</body>
</html>
```

In the code, we accept two numbers using a html form. The two numbers are

assigned to two variables n1 and n2.

Then we calculate the sum, difference, product and quotient and assign them

to 4 different variables.

At the end, these 4 variables are printed out using document.write()

Output:

Enter First Number: 3
Enter Second Number: 5

Calculate

The sum is 8
The difference is -2
The product is 15
The quotient is 0.6

Modulus Operation

The modulus operation returns the remainder between two numbers. It looks like the percentage sign %. Here's an example below:

```html
<html>
 <head><title>Sample Form</title></head>
 <body>
 <form id="form1">
 Enter First Number:<input name="number1" type="number" id="num1" size="20"><br>
 Enter Second Number:<input name="number2" type="number" id="num2" size="20"><br><br>

 <button onclick="test()">Calculate Remainder</button>

 <script>
 function test()
 {
 var n1 = parseInt(document.getElementById("num1").value);
 var n2 = parseInt(document.getElementById("num2").value);
 var remainder=n1%n2;

 document.write("The remainder when "+n1+"is divided by "+n2+" is "+remainder+"<br>");

 }
 </script>

 </body>
</html>
```

The above code takes in two numbers via a html form and finds the remainder between the two; as shown in output below.

Output:

Enter First Number: 17

Enter Second Number: 6

Calculate Remainder

After hitting the button **"Calculate Remainder"**

The remainder when 17 is divided by 6 is 5

Math.Random()

Math.Random() returns a random number between 0 and 1. If we want to get a random between 0 and 10, we multiply by 10 and round the answer (using Math.round()). Let's look at a few examples.

```
<html>
  <head><title>Sample Form</title></head>
  <body>

  <button onclick="test()">Random Numbers</button>

  <script>
  function test()
  {
  var n1 = Math.random();
  var n2 = Math.round(Math.random()*50);
  var n3 = Math.round(Math.random()*50);
  var n4 = Math.round(Math.random()*1000);

  var remainder=n1%n2;

  document.write("Random number between 0 and 1 = <strong>"+n1+"</strong><br>");
  document.write("1st Random number between 0 and 50 = <strong>"+n2+"</strong><br>");
  document.write("2nd Random number between 0 and 50 = <strong>"+n3+"</strong><br>");
  document.write("Random number between 0 and 1000 = <strong>"+n4+"</strong><br>");


  }
  </script>

  </body>
</html>
```

In the above example, n1 is a random number between 0 and 1.

n2 and n3 are two different random numbers between 0 and 50. You should

probably see that n2 and n3 are different because both numbers are

randomized.

n4 returns a random number between 0 and 1000.

We can see the results in the output below. As the numbers are randomized

we should get a different result each time we run the program.

Math.Random() is a fun function and we are going to be using it in quite a

few games this book.

Output:

```
Random number between 0 and 1 = 0.20604429056114348
1st Random number between 0 and 50 = 21
2nd Random number between 0 and 50 = 6
Random number between 0 and 1000 = 866
```

Exponent and Logarithms

Exponents in Javascript are done using the Math.pow() function and natural logarithms are done using Math.log(). If we want logarithm to the base 10 we use Math.log10().

```
<html>
<head><title>Sample Form</title></head>
<body>

<button onclick="test()">Random Numbers</button>

<script>
function test()
{
var n1 = Math.pow(6,2);
var n2 = Math.pow(7,3);
var n3 = Math.log(100);
var n4 = Math.log10(100);

document.write("6 raised to the power 2 = <strong>"+n1+"</strong><br>");
document.write("7 raised to the power 3 = <strong>"+n2+"</strong><br>");
document.write("The natural logarithm of 100 is = <strong>"+n3+"</strong><br>");
document.write("Logarithm (to the base 10) of 100 is = <strong>"+n4+"</strong><br>");

}
</script>

</body>
</html>
```

In the code above, we have two examples of exponents using Math.pow(x,y). Basically, x is raised to the power of y in both both cases. n1 and n2 give exponents. n3 shows a natural logarithm of 100 and n4 shows logarithm to base 10 of 100.

Output:

6 raised to the power 2 = **36**

7 raised to the power 3 = **343**

The natural logarithm of 100 is = **4.605170185988092**

Logarithm (to the base 10) of 100 is = **2**

Square root

Math.sqrt() is used the find square root and Math.Abs() is used to find the absolute value of a number.

Here's a few examples:

```
<html>
 <head><title>Sample Form</title></head>
<body>

 <button onclick="test()">Test</button>

<script>
 function test()
{
 var n1 = Math.sqrt(36);
 var n2 = Math.sqrt(75);
 var n3 = Math.abs(13);
 var n4 = Math.abs(-14);

 document.write("The square root of 36 = <strong>"+n1+"</strong><br>");
 document.write("The square root of 75 = <strong>"+n2+"</strong><br>");
 document.write("The absolute value of 13 is = <strong>"+n3+"</strong><br>");
 document.write("The absolute value of -14 = <strong>"+n4+"</strong><br>");


}
</script>

</body>
</html>
```

In the above code, n1 and n2 are examples of the square root function; while

n3 and n4 are examples of the absolute function.

If you haven't heard of the absolute value function, it basically returns a

positive value whether the number is +ve or -ve. So, 13 and -13 would both

return an absolute value of 13.

Output:

```
The square root of 36 = 6
The square root of 75 = 8.660254037844387
The absolute value of 13 is = 13
The absolute value of -14 = 14
```

Trigonometry

Yes, JavaScript can be used for trigonometric functions as well. Here's a few of them.

Math.sin(x) returns the sine value of x radians. If we want to find the sine of x degrees, then we have to convert it to radians. So, we should change the function to Math.sin(x*MATH.PI/180).

Also, keep in mind that in Javascript, we represent the value of π as Math.PI

We can also do cos and tan function using Math.cos(x) and Math.tan(x), where x is in radians.

Let's look at an example program below:

```
<html>
<head><title>Sample Form</title></head>
<body>

<button onclick="test()">Test</button>

<script>
function test()
{
var n1 = Math.sin(5);
var n2 = Math.sin(5*Math.PI/180);
var n3 = Math.sin(90*Math.PI/180);
var n4 = Math.cos(10);
var n5 = Math.cos(10*Math.PI/180);
var n6 = Math.cos(0*Math.PI/180);
var n7 = Math.tan(30);
var n8 = Math.tan(30*Math.PI/180);
var n9 = Math.tan(45*Math.PI/180);

document.write("The sine of 5 radians = <strong>"+n1+"</strong><br>");
document.write("The sine of 5 degrees = <strong>"+n2+"</strong><br>");
document.write("The sine of 90 degrees = <strong>"+n3+"</strong><br>");
document.write("The cos of 10 radians = <strong>"+n1+"</strong><br>");
document.write("The cos of 10 degrees = <strong>"+n2+"</strong><br>");
document.write("The cos of 0 degrees = <strong>"+n3+"</strong><br>");
document.write("The tan of 30 radians = <strong>"+n7+"</strong><br>");
document.write("The tan of 30 degrees = <strong>"+n8+"</strong><br>");
document.write("The tan of 45 degrees = <strong>"+n9+"</strong><br>");

}
</script>

</body>
</html>
```

In the above code, we show 3 examples of sine, cos and tan values. And we show the difference between calculating trigonometric values of degrees and radians. For example, for n1, we calculate the value of sin(5 radians) and in n2 we calculate the value of sin(5 degrees). In n2, we had to convert 5 degrees into radians by doing sin(5* π/180).

Output:

```
The sine of 5 radians = -0.9589242746631385
The sine of 5 degrees = 0.08715574274765817
The sine of 90 degrees = 1
The cos of 10 radians = -0.9589242746631385
The cos of 10 degrees = 0.08715574274765817
The cos of 0 degrees = 1
The tan of 30 radians = -6.405331196646276
The tan of 30 degrees = 0.5773502691896257
The tan of 45 degrees = 0.9999999999999999
```

Practice Problems

1. Write a program that calculates the total salary payment cost for a team. Create a form that takes in two inputs; number of employees and average hours worked per employee. Use parseInt to ensure that the number of employees is an integer. Round the average hours worked to the top hour (So, 5.2 and 5.6 hours would both become 6 hours). Multiply the two inputs and print out the total salary paid to employees.

2. Let's get started and make a demo calculator with all that we've learned. Create a form that takes in two numbers in 2 textboxs and has 15 buttons. Each buttons links to a JavaScript button that does a calculation. Create a button each for addition, subtraction, multiplication, division, remainder, exponent, natural logarithms, logarithms (to base 10), square root, sine, cos, tan, cosec, sec, cot. Some of these buttons only need one number to operate (trig functions, square root, logarithms) while others need two numbers.

3. Create a program that calculates the height of a building you are looking at using trigonometry. The program takes in two user inputs

in a form. The first is the distance from the building; and the second

is the viewing angle to the top of the building. Use trigonometry (tan

value to be specific) to calculate the height of the building.

Loops

Loops in coding are a sequence of instructions that are repeated a certain number of times.

Think of a loop like an escalator. The steps run in a direction again and again till someone pushes the stop button.

There are 3 types of loops based on the conditions of execution. They are:

a. **IF Loops:** IF loops contain a sequence of instructions that are executed if a certain condition is met. If the conditions are not met, the loop is not executed.

b. **FOR Loops:** FOR loops contain a sequence of instructions that are executed for a certain number of times. For example, a FOR loop from 1 to 10 executes the code inside the loop 10 times.

c. **WHILE Loops:** WHILE loops is a sequence of instructions that are executed till a certain condition is met.

Now, let's look at the elevator example through each of these loops.

Let's say we want the elevator to run only when there are more than 1000 people in the building. Then we use an IF loop that checks the number of people in the building and then runs the elevator function if that is the case.

The IF Loop Example:

```
if(people>1000)

{

Runelevator();

}
```

Now, if we want to do a 1000 run test on the elevator to see if it can hold a certain weight; we use a FOR loop. The FOR loop below starts at 0 and ends at 999, thus running the elevator a 1000 times.

```
for (i=0;i<1000;i++)

{

Runelevator();

}
```

Finally, if we want to keep running the elevator till 6 PM, we use a WHILE loop.

```
While (checktime!=18:00)

{

Runelevator();

}
```

These are simple examples of the 3 loops to explain the concepts of loops. This concept is very important in coding.

Now, let's do some examples in JavaScript.

IF LOOP EXAMPLE 1

IF loops are also called conditionals. A conditional is a piece of code that checks if a certain condition has been fulfilled. For example, an insurance company might want to give you a lower rate if the combined ages of your two kids is higher than 15. So, you check for those condition. Let's look at it using an IF loop below.

```
<html>
<head><title>Insurance Test</title></head>
<body>
Enter Age of 1st Kid:<input name="a1" type="number" id="age1" size="20"><br>
Enter Age of 2nd Kid:<input name="a2" type="number" id="age2" size="20"><br><br>

<button onclick="checkinsuranceprice()">Check Price</button>

<script>
function checkinsuranceprice()
{
var inscost=0;
var a1 = parseInt(document.getElementById("age1").value);
var a2 = parseInt(document.getElementById("age2").value);

//Check condition
if ((a1+a2)>15)
{
inscost=inscost+300;
}
else
{
inscost=inscost+600;
}
document.write("Your annual car insurance is $"+inscost);
}
</script>

</body>
</html>
```

In the above a html form allows the user to enter two ages with ids' "age1" and "age2". The JavaScript variables a1 and a2 store the values of the variables. The IF statement checks if the sum of the two is greater than 15. If it's greater than 15, insurance cost is $300; otherwise it's $600. Finally, we print out the value of the insurance. Here's the output below.

Output #1:

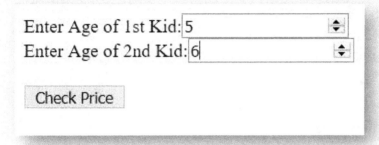

On clicking **Check Price**:

Your annual car insurance is $600

Output #2:

Enter Age of 1st Kid: 5

Enter Age of 2nd Kid: 12

Check Price

On clicking **Check Price**:

Your annual car insurance is $300

IF LOOP EXAMPLE 2

Let's take another example. How about if you are looking to figure out which

gym to sign up for. You want to sign up for gyms that are within 5 miles and

cost less than $60 per month. So, you have two IF loops that check for each

condition. The loops are within each other. This is called a Nested Loop. Let's

have a look below.

```html
<html>
<head><title>Gym Test</title></head>
<body>
Enter Name of Gym:<input name="g1" type="text" id="gname" size="20"><br>
Enter Gym Distance from home:<input name="g2" type="number" id="dist" size="20"><br>
Enter Monthly Membership Costs:<input name="g3" type="number" id="memc" size="20"><br><br>

<button onclick="checkgym()">Check Gym</button>

<script>
function checkgym()
{
var name = document.getElementById("gname").value;
var gymdistance = parseInt(document.getElementById("dist").value);
var memberprice = parseInt(document.getElementById("memc").value);

//Check condition
if (gymdistance<5)
{
    if(memberprice<60)
    {
    document.write(name+" is a possible gym");
    }
    else
    {
    document.write(name+" does not work for me");
    }
}
else
{
    document.write(name+" does not work for me");
}
}
</script>

</body>
</html>
```

In the above a html form allows the user to enter a gym name with id="gname", a gymdistance with id="dist" and a gym price with id="memc". The JavaScript variables name, gymdistance and memberprice store the values of the user inputs. One IF statement checks if gymdistance is less than 5. If it's greater than 5, the gym is not good. If it's less than 5, then we use another IF to check if monthly membership price is less than $60. If yes, then this is one possible gym; otherwise it is no good. Here's a few sample outputs below.

Output #1:

Enter Name of Gym: First Fitness
Enter Gym Distance from home: 6
Enter Monthly Membership Costs: 40

Check Gym

Fitness First does not work for me

Output #2:

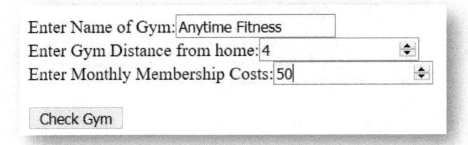

Enter Name of Gym: Anytime Fitness
Enter Gym Distance from home: 4
Enter Monthly Membership Costs: 50

Check Gym

Anytime Fitness is a possible gym

Output #3:

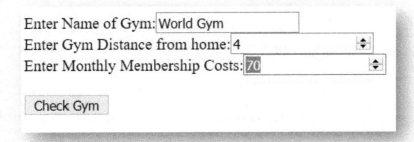

Enter Name of Gym: World Gym
Enter Gym Distance from home: 4
Enter Monthly Membership Costs: 70

Check Gym

FOR LOOP Example 1

A simple example of a For Loop is a program that counts to 10.

```html
<html>
<head><title>Loops......</title></head>
<body>

  <button onclick="printtoten()">Print To 10</button>

<script>

 function printtoten()
 {

 for (i=1;i<=10;i++)
 {
     document.write(i+"<br>");
 }
 }

</script>

</body>
</html>
```

The above code is a simple example of a for loop. It has a button that runs

the function printten(). Printtoten() has a for loop that prints numbers 1 to 10

on the screen through document.write().

106

The line above means that the loop starts from 1 (i=1). It is increasing by 1 each time (i++). The loop ends when i reaches 10 (i<=10).

Output:

Once you click the button on the output, you see the numbers 1 to 10 printed on the screen.

Print To 10

```
1
2
3
4
5
6
7
8
9
10
```

FOR LOOP Example 2

Now, let's do a slightly different version of this. In this example, we're going to use a form that takes in a number for the loop. That means we can make the loop as long as we want.

```html
<html>
<head><title>Loops......</title></head>
<body>

<form id="form1">
How long do you want the loop?: <input name="Loop Number" type="number" id="loop" size="20"><br>

</form>

<button onclick="printtoten()">Print To 10</button>
<button onclick="printlooplength()">Print Loop Length</button>

<script>

function printtoten()
{

for (i=1;i<=10;i++)
{
    document.write(i+"<br>");
}
}
function printlooplength()
{
var looplength=parseInt(document.getElementById("loop").value);

for (i=1;i<=looplength;i++)
{
    document.write(i+"<br>");
}
}
</script>

</body>
</html>
```

A html form was added to this program

The form takes in a number input and stores in a variable called **"loop"**.

There is a second button labelled **"Print Loop Length"** which runs the

"printlooplength()" function.

In the function, we assign the form variable "loop" to another variable

"looplength". And we run the loop from 1 to **"looplength"**. The loop prints

the numbers between 1 and **"looplength"**.

In the example below, we put 35 in the form; and as we can see, it prints out

numbers between 1 and 35.

How long do you want the loop?: 35

Print To 10   Print Loop Length

1
2
3
4
5
6
7
8
9
10
11
12
13
14
15
16
17
18
19
20
21
22
23
24
25
26
27
28
29
30
31
32
33
34
35

FOR Loop Example 3 – Nested Loops

In the final example, we use FOR loops to create a star pattern.

So, we create a 2nd button labelled 'Print Star Loop' which runs **starloop()** on clicking. In the function, again, looplength has the value of the loop we enter in the form.

So, first, we create a FOR loop that goes from 1 to looplength. The variable i holds the count value of the loop and increases by 1 each time.

Then, we create another FOR loop within that goes from 1 to i. The second FOR loop prints the star("*") i times.

So, for example, if you're going through the first loop for the 5th time, i=5. The second loop prints * from 1 to 5 (i.e. 5 times).

In the example, below, we print the star loop for a looplength of 23.

Output

```html
<html>
<head><title>Loops......</title></head>
<body>
<form id="form1">
Loop Number: <input name="Loop Number" type="number" id="loop" size="20"><br>
</form>
<button class="btn printoten" onclick="printtoten()">Print To 10</button>
<button class="btn printoten" onclick="printlooplength()">Print Loop Length</button>
<button class="btn printoten" onclick="starloop()">Print Star Loop</button>
<script>

function printtoten()
{
for (i=1;i<=10;i++)
{
    document.write(i+"<br>");
}
}
function printlooplength()
{
var looplength=parseInt(document.getElementById("loop").value);

for (i=1;i<=looplength;i++)
{
    document.write(i+"<br>");
}
}
function starloop()
{
var looplength=parseInt(document.getElementById("loop").value);

for (i=1;i<=looplength;i++)
    {
    for (j=1;j<=i;j++)
    {
    document.write("*");
    }
    document.write("<br>");
    }
}
</script>
</body>
</html>
```

Loop Number: 23

Print To 10   Print Loop Length   Print Star Loop

```
*
**
***
****
*****
******
*******
********
*********
**********
***********
************
*************
**************
***************
****************
*****************
******************
*******************
********************
*********************
**********************
***********************
************************
```

WHILE LOOP EXAMPLE 1

A while loop runs while a certain condition is met. If the condition is no longer met, it breaks out of the loop. In the below example, the program executes a while loop that takes in a user input via the prompt function. The while loop keeps running and printing the user text. The loop stops when the user inputs the word **'STOP'**. Once the word is input, that's the end of the while loops and the program stops.

```
<html>
 <head><title>While Loop Test</title></head>
<body>

 <button onclick="testwhileloop()">Test</button>

<script>
 function testwhileloop()
{
 var inputtext = "";
 while (inputtext != "STOP")
{
    inputtext = prompt("Enter what you want to do now (Enter in ALL CAPS");
    document.write("Next Activity = "+inputtext+"<br>");
-}

-}
-</script>

-</body>
-</html>
```

Here's the output below that shows how this works.

Output:

```
Next Activity = TENNIS
Next Activity = FOOTBALL
Next Activity = STOP
```

Practice Problems

1. Write a program that inputs a number via a form and checks if its

   divisible by 3.

2. Write a program that takes a user input and outputs the following

   pattern below. For example, if the user inputs the number '5' it

   outputs:

1

22

333

4444

55555

3. Write a program that takes in seven user inputs that are different

   animals. Then write a function that checks if any of these animals is a

   tiger, and then print out which number animal is the tiger.

4. Write a program that is a filter for a car dealership. It takes in the

   name and price of a car via prompt function. The program prints out the name of the car each time. It stops when the sum of all the cars exceed a value of $50000; as that is the upper limit of their budget.

5. Write a program that takes in two user number inputs via prompt function. Keep making the user input two numbers till their sum is greater than 20. Once the user inputs two numbers whose sum is greater than 20, the program stops.

6. Write a program that takes in the vote of a person via user prompt. There are 3 candidates. It checks if the vote is any of the candidates and adds to the candidate vote total. There is a final prompt that asks if there are any more votes and it accepts the values of 'Y/N'. If 'N', then it stops the program and prints out the winner. If 'Y', then it asks for the vote again and repeats the process.

7. Write a program that takes a user input and outputs the following star pattern below. For example, if the user inputs the number '6' it outputs:

```
******
*****
****
***
```

**

*

8. Write a program that takes in a user input and prints out the sum of numbers from 1 to that number. For example, if the user inputs 3; the sum is 1+2+3=6.

Game Time - Loops

Now, it's time to design a few games based on what we've learned so far.

There's no better way of learning concepts than applying them; and even better to apply them to something fun.

Before, getting started, let's talk about one concept; which is adding html elements using Javascript.

Adding html Elements using JavaScript

What if want to add a button or textbox in the middle of the JavaScript program. Yes, you can do that within JavaScript using the document.write() function. For example, you can create a button using:

```
document.write('<button onClick="afunction()">Restart</button>');
```

In the above line, we create a button with text 'Restart' on it. On clicking the button, **afunction()** is run. This is very useful in games where we have the option to keep running the program instead of stopping. Now, let's look at a similar program below.

```html
<html>
<head><title>Sample Form</title></head>
<body>
<link rel="stylesheet" type="text/css" href="samplestyle.css" />
<form id="form1">
Enter First Number:<input name="number1" type="number" id="num1" size="20"><br>
Enter Second Number:<input name="number2" type="number" id="num2" size="20"><br><br>
Enter Third Number: <input name="number3" type="number" id="num3" size="20"></textarea><br><br>

<button class = "btn submit" onclick="multiplynum()">Submit</button>

<script>
function multiplynum()
{
var n1 = document.getElementById("num1").value;
var n2 = document.getElementById("num2").value;
var n3 = document.getElementById("num3").value;
document.write('<link rel="stylesheet" type="text/css" href="samplestyle.css" />');
document.write("The product of the three numbers is " +n1*n2*n3);
document.write('<br>');
document.write('<button onclick="redirect()">Home</button>');


function redirect()
{
window.location.replace("form_JavaScript.html");
}

</script>

</body>
</html>
```

The program above is the form in the previous chapter. We just added two

lines and a function.

The two lines create a Home button which runs the function **redirect()**.

The **redirect()** function runs the program again. **'form_JavaScript.html'** is the

name of the file we are running. You should change 'form_JavaScript' to

whatever you have named your html file.

Output #1

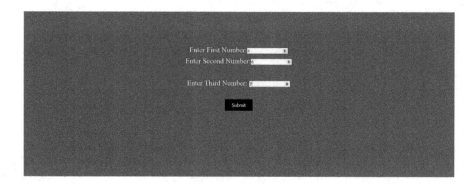

After entering numbers and clicking Submit, we get:

The Product Of The Three Numbers Is 168

Home

And now, after clicking Home button, we get:

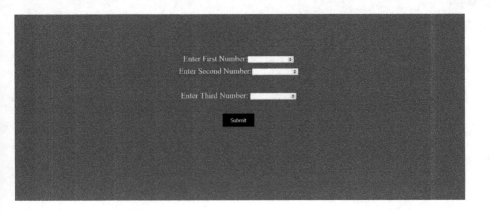

So, it basically restarts the html program.

Now, let's get started with our first game.

Game 1 – Guess Random Numbers

In this game, we're going to create a form that takes in a number via a textbox. The number is between 0 and 10. Then we compare that number to a random number generated via JavaScript (using Math.random). If it is the same, then the guessed number is correct. If not, then we give them the right number. The user has the option to click the Home button and try again. See the code and output below.

```html
<html>
<head><title>Guess Number</title>
<link rel="stylesheet" href="samplestyle.css" />
</head>
<body>
<form id="form1">
Guess Number between 0 and 10:<input name="name" type="number" id="num1" size="20"><br>
</form>
<button class="btn a" onclick="guessnumber()">Check</button>
<script>

function guessnumber()
{
var guess=document.getElementById("num1").value;
var rand=Math.floor(Math.random()*10);
if (guess==rand)
{
    document.write("Congratulations. You guessed the right number");
}else{
    document.write("Sorry. You guessed wrong. The correct number is "+rand);
}

document.write('<link rel="stylesheet" type="text/css" href="samplestyle.css" />');
document.write('<br>');
document.write('<button onClick="redirect()">Home</button>');


}
function redirect()
{
window.location.replace("GuessNumber.html");
}

</script>

</body>
</html>
```

Output:

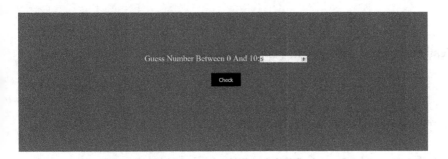

If we click **Home**, we can play the game again.

This program is a good way to practice conditional loops and random number generators.

Game 2 – Math Quiz Game

This is a bit of a longer program, so I've broken it up into 2 pictures. It basically prints out 5 simple math problems and takes in answers to these problems via a form (they have id's of **num1,num2,num3,num4,num5**). The answers are stored as variables in JavaScript **(answer1,answer2,answer3,answer4,answer5).** These answers are compared to the real answers using IF functions. A counter is incremented by 1 each time the user gets a correct answer and finally the counter is printed to see how many correct answers the user got.

```html
<html>
 <head><title>Math Quiz</title></head>
 <link rel="stylesheet" href="samplestyles.css" />
 <body>
 <form id="form1">
 5*2 = :<input name="name" type="number" id="num1" size="20"><br>
 7/2 = :<input name="name" type="float" id="num2" size="20"><br>
 6*5 = :<input name="name" type="number" id="num3" size="20"><br>
 14+29 = :<input name="name" type="number" id="num4" size="20"><br>
 17-6 = :<input name="name" type="number" id="num5" size="20"><br>
 </form>
 <button class="btn" onclick="guessnumber()">Check</button>
 <script>

 function guessnumber()
 {
 var correct=0;

 var answer1=parseInt(document.getElementById("num1").value);
 var answer2=parseFloat(document.getElementById("num2").value);
 var answer3=parseInt(document.getElementById("num3").value);
 var answer4=parseInt(document.getElementById("num4").value);
 var answer5=parseInt(document.getElementById("num5").value);
```

```javascript
if (answer1==10)
{
    correct=correct+1;
}
if (answer2==3.5)
{
    correct=correct+1;
}
if (answer3==30)
{
    correct=correct+1;
}
if (answer4==43)
{
    correct=correct+1;
}
if (answer5==11)
{
    correct=correct+1;
}
document.write('<link rel="stylesheet" type="text/css" href="samplestyle.css" />');
document.write("You got "+correct+" answers correct");
}

</script>

</body>
</html>
```

Output:

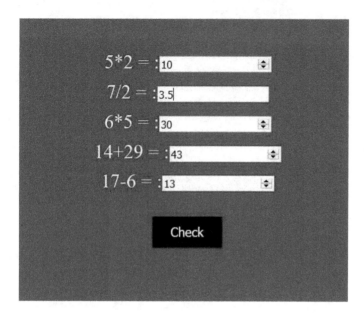

On clicking **Check** button, we get:

> You Got 5 Answers Correct

This is a great practice program. But you might be thinking that kids can use this program only once as we always use the same numbers. To fix this problem, we generate random numbers in the next game.

Game 3 – Math Quiz with Random Numbers

In this program below, there are 5 math questions generated by 10 random numbers. The 10 random numbers are variables **number1-number10**. The answers to the questions are calculated and are stored in variables **answer1-answer5**. These 15 variables are called global variables as they are outside any functions. This means that their values can be accessed anywhere in the program by any function.

The function **startquiz()** uses the 10 variables **number1-number10** to write the quiz on the screen and create a form that takes in 5 answers with id's **num1-num5**. On clicking the **Check** button, these 5 answers are sent to the function **guessnumber()** and stored as variables **guess1-guess5**. These 5 answers **(guess1-guess5)** are checked against calculated answers **(answer1-answer5)** using 5 different IF functions. Each time there is a correct answer, a counter is incremented. Eventually, the counter is printed to show the number of correct answers. There is also a **Home** button at the end which gives the user the option to restart the program with fresh questions.

These questions are randomly generated which means that the user gets different questions each time.

```html
<html>
<head><title>Math Quiz</title></head>
<link rel="stylesheet" href="samplestyle.css" />
<body>
<button class="btn" onclick="startquiz()">Start Math Quiz</button>

<script>

var number1=Math.floor(Math.random()*10)+1;
var number2=Math.floor(Math.random()*10)+1;
var number3=Math.floor(Math.random()*10)+1;
var number4=Math.floor(Math.random()*10)+1;
var number5=Math.floor(Math.random()*50)+1;
var number6=Math.floor(Math.random()*50)+1;
var number7=Math.floor(Math.random()*50)+1;
var number8=Math.floor(Math.random()*50)+1;
var number9=Math.floor(Math.random()*50)+1;
var number10=Math.floor(Math.random()*50)+1;
var answer1=number1*number2;
var answer2=number3*number4;
var answer3=number5+number6;
var answer4=number7-number8;
var answer5=number9%number10;

function startquiz()
{
document.write(number1+" * "+number2+" = ");
document.write('<input name="name" type="number" id="num1" size="20"><br>');

document.write(number3+" * "+number4+" = ");
document.write('<input name="name" type="number" id="num2" size="20"><br>');

document.write(number5+" + "+number6+" = ");
document.write('<input name="name" type="number" id="num3" size="20"><br>');

document.write(number7+" - "+number8+" = ");
document.write('<input name="name" type="number" id="num4" size="20"><br>');

document.write(number9+" / "+number10+". Remainder= ");
document.write('<input name="name" type="number" id="num5" size="20"><br>');
document.write('<link rel="stylesheet" type="text/css" href="samplestyle.css" />');
document.write('<br>');
document.write('<button class="btn a" onclick="guessnumber()">Check</button><br>');
}
```

130

```
function guessnumber()
{
document.body.innerhtml='';
correctanswers=0;
var guess1=document.getElementById("num1").value;
var guess2=document.getElementById("num2").value;
var guess3=document.getElementById("num3").value;
var guess4=document.getElementById("num4").value;
var guess5=document.getElementById("num5").value;
document.write("Answer 1 = "+answer1+'<br>');
document.write("Answer 2 = "+answer2+'<br>');
document.write("Answer 3 = "+answer3+'<br>');
document.write("Answer 4 = "+answer4+'<br>');
document.write("Answer 5 = "+answer5+'<br>');

if (guess1==answer1)
{
    correctanswers=correctanswers+1;
}
if (guess2==answer2)
{
    correctanswers=correctanswers+1;
}
if (guess3==answer3)
{
    correctanswers=correctanswers+1;
}
if (guess4==answer4)
{
    correctanswers=correctanswers+1;
}
if (guess5==answer5)
{
    correctanswers=correctanswers+1;
}

document.write("Number of correct answers = "+correctanswers);
document.write('<br>');
document.write('<button class="btn a" onClick="redirect()">Home</button>');

}
```

```
document.write("Number of correct answers = "+correctanswers);
document.write('<br>');
document.write('<button class="btn a" onClick="redirect()">Home</button>');

}


function redirect()
{
window.location.replace("MathQuiz_Random_Numbers.html");
}

</script>

</body>
</html>
```

Output:

On clicking **Check** button, we get:

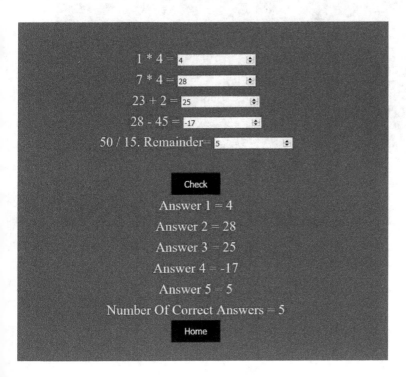

Now, we know that we got all correct answers. Now, let's click **Home** again.

We click **Start Math Quiz** to get us here again to do another quiz again. Since the numbers are randomized, we get 5 completely different questions.

Brilliant!!

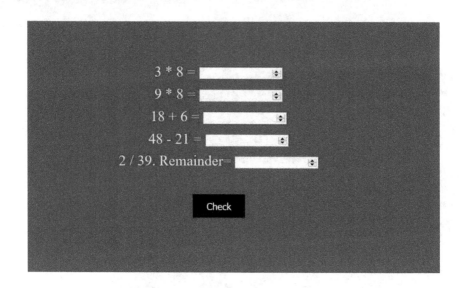

3 * 8 = [▲▼]

9 * 8 = [▲▼]

18 + 6 = [▲▼]

48 - 21 = [▲▼]

2 / 39. Remainder= [▲▼]

Check

Practice Problems

1. Write a program that generates two random numbers between 0 and 10. The program calculates their sum and product. It prints out the sum and product on the screen and asks the user to guess the 2 numbers. The user inputs his guesses through a form and it is checked against the initial two numbers. If he gets it right, then he gets a congratulatory message. If he gets it wrong, the program lets him know the correct answers. At the end, there is the option to restart the program and try again.

2. Write a program that generates a random number between 0 and 20. It squares the number and prints the square on the screen. Then, it asks the user to guess what the number is. The user inputs the number via a form and the program checks whether it is correct or not.

3. Write a program that allows the user to input 3 numbers via a form. These 3 numbers are supposed to be the 3 sides of a triangle. The program then checks if this is a right-angled triangle. The program lets the user know if it is a right-angled triangle (Hint: Use Pythagros theorem to check).

String Variables

A string variable in JavaScript programming is used to store a group of characters.

For example:

```
var x="awe3t5"
```

x is a string variable that stores the value of "awe3t5".

It is a string variable of size 6. When we access the string, remember that the values start from 0 instead of 1. For example, x[0] returns a value of a, x[1] returns w and so on.

Strings are very useful in processing text information likes names, addresses etc.

Here's a list of useful functions that can be used to process strings.

length – This returns the length of a string. In the above example, x.length returns 6.

charAt(y) – This returns the character at position y in the string. For example, in the string x; if we want the 5th character, we do x.charAt(5) and that returns t.

indexOf(y) – Checks the index of character y in the string. For example, x.indexOf('a') returns 0.

lastIndexOf(y) – Checks the last index of character y in the string. For example, x.lastIndexOf('e') returns 3. This is only useful if there are multiple occurrences of the same string.

.concat(b) – This join string b to a previous string. For example, if string a = "xyz" and string b = "lmn"; a.concat(b) gives "xyzlmn".

includes(y) – This checks if string y is included in a string and returns a true or false value. For example, if string x= "Hi Peter"; then x.includes("Hi") returns true, but x.includes("Home") returns false.

replace(x,a) – This basically replaces all instances of string x with string a. For example if a string str ="Hi Peter"; then str.replace("Hi","Hello") becomes str="Hello Peter".

startswith(y) – This checks if a string starts with string y. It returns a Boolean variable of **true** or **false** value. In the above example, str.startswith("Hi") returns true while str.startswith("Hello") returns false.

toUpper() – This changes the entire string to upper case. In the above example, str.toUpper() becomes "HI PETER".

toLower() – This changes the entire string to lower case. In the above example, str.Lower() becomes "hi peter".

Example 1 – Playing with Your Name; Reverse name game

In the example below, we enter our name through a form. There are two buttons, one prints the length of your name; and the second reverses your name. The first button runs a function called **strlength()**. **strlength()** gets your name via the form and finds the length using the **.length** function.

The second button executes a function called **namereverse()**. namereverse() gets your name via the form again and finds the length. Then it runs a FOR loop which starts from the last character and keeps subtracting 1 till it reaches the first character. It prints out the character at each loop iteration.

138

This prints out letters from the last character to the first, thus reversing the name.

Below is the code and output.

```html
<html>
 <head><title>JavaScript Lesson 4 - Strings</title></head>
<body>
 <link rel="stylesheet" href="samplestyle.css" />
<form id="form1">
 Enter Name:<input name="name" type="text" id="name" size="20"><br>

 <button onclick="strlength()">Name Length</button>
 <button onclick="namereverse()">Name Reverse</button>

<script>

 function strlength()
{
 var nm=document.getElementById("name").value;
 document.write("Your name is "+nm.length+ " characters long");
 document.write('<link rel="stylesheet" type="text/css" href="samplestyle.css" />');
 document.write('<br>');
 }

 function namereverse()
{
 var nm=document.getElementById("name").value;
 len=nm.length;
 document.write("Name Reversed = ");
 for (i=len-1;i>=0;i--)
{
 document.write(nm[i]);
 }
 document.write('<link rel="stylesheet" type="text/css" href="samplestyle.css" />');
 document.write('<br>');
 }

</script>

</body>
</html>
```

139

Output:

Enter Name: Mather

Name Length   Name Reverse

On Clicking **Name Length**

Your Name Is 6 Characters Long

On Clicking **Name Reverse**

Name Reversed = RehtaM

Example 2 –Address Check

In the below program, the user enters a name and an address via a form. The address is entered via a textarea to allow for larger number of characters. It accepts 5 rows of 40 characters each (200 characters in total). So, the goal of this program is to assign all New York residents flying in to a separate hotel. The button runs a function called addcheck(). Addcheck() takes in name and address from the form and assigns them to variables.

An IF function with .includes() checks if the address contains "New York". If it does, then the name string concatenates with the hotel 1 string using .concat().

If it does not contain New York, then the name string concatenates with the hotel 2 string.

We print out the concatenated string in either case.

Here's the code with a couple of outputs below showcasing the 2 different cases.

```html
<html>
<head><title>JavaScript Lesson 4 - Strings</title></head>
<body>
<link rel="stylesheet" href="samplestyle.css" />
<form id="form1">
Enter Name:<input name="name" type="text" id="name" size="20"><br>
Enter Address: <textarea name="TextBox" cols="40" rows="5" id="address"></textarea><br><br>


<button onclick="addcheck()">Check Address</button>

<script>

function addcheck()
{
var nm=document.getElementById("name").value;
var address=document.getElementById("address").value;
var len=address.length;
var pstr="";
h1=" stays in Hotel 1";
h2=" stays in Hotel 2";
if (address.includes("New York"))
{
pstr=nm.concat(h1);
document.write(pstr);
}
else
{
pstr=nm.concat(h2);
document.write(pstr);
}
document.write('<link rel="stylesheet" type="text/css" href="samplestyle.css" />');
document.write('<br>');
}


</script>


</body>
</html>
```

Output #1:

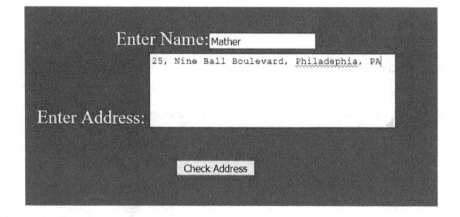

On Clicking **Check Address**, it shows Hotel 2 because address is not from New York.

Output #2

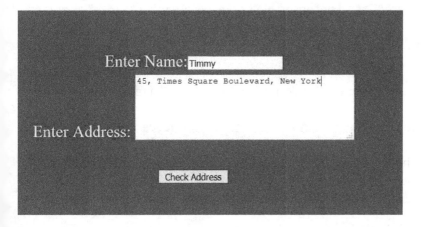

On Clicking **Check Address**, it shows Hotel 1 because address is a New York address.

Timmy Stays In Hotel 1

Example 3 – Enter a string and replace all curse words with *****

In the below code, we input a text via textarea and replace all curse words with five stars *****. For censorship's sake, we are using **"Fudge"** as our curse word.

The button runs **filterc()** function. The **filterc()** function takes in the text via the textarea id in the form. An IF function with **.includes** and **.toUpperCase()** checks if the word "Fudge" is found. The **.toUpperCase()** is used because we do not know if the curse word is entered in lower case or Upper case.

If it is the curse word, we use **.replace** to replace the words "Fudge" and "FUDGE" with "*****". At the end, we print out the modified string. We have the code and a couple of output variations below.

```
<html>
<head><title>JavaScript Lesson 4 - Strings</title></head>
<body>
<link rel="stylesheet" href="samplestyle.css" />
<form id="form1">
Enter Name:<input name="name" type="text" id="name" size="20"><br>
Enter Text: <textarea name="TextBox" cols="40" rows="5" id="phrase"></textarea><br><br>


<button onclick="filterc()">Filter Curse Words</button>

<script>

function filterc()
{
var nm=document.getElementById("name").value;
var text=document.getElementById("phrase").value;
var modtext=text;
if (text.toUpperCase().includes("FUDGE"))
{
modtext=text.replace("Fudge","*****").replace("FUDGE","*****");
}
document.write("Modified Text ="+modtext);
document.write('<link rel="stylesheet" type="text/css" href="samplestyle.css" />');
document.write('<br>');
}

</script>

</body>
</html>
```

Output #1:

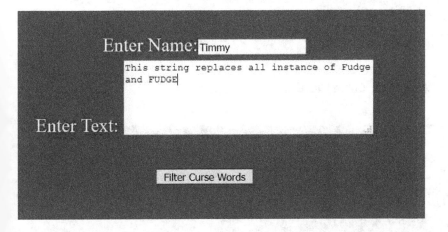

On Clicking **Filter Curse Words**...

Modified Text =This String Replaces All Instance Of **** And *****

Output #2:

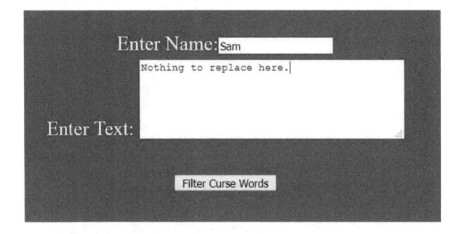

On Clicking **Filter Curse Words**...

Modified Text =Nothing To Replace Here.

Practice Problems

1. Write a program that takes in a string and prints out every 2nd character in the string. For example "wfwfwkfnfwbej" would print out "ffkbwj".

2. Write a program that takes in a long sentence and replaces all instances of the word "red" with "yellow".

3. Write a program that takes in an address and checks if the zip code contains 5 characters. If it contains more or less, or there is no zip code, print out "Invalid Address".

Arrays

An array in JavaScript is used to store a group of similar variables.

Think about how you would store ages of people using variables. Let's say we have three people and their ages. We can store them in variables age1; age2 and age 3.

```
age1=5;
```

```
age2=25;
```

```
age=45;
```

Now, let's say we have 10 people. We can store it in variables age1, age2…..age10. Now, what if we had to store it for 100 people. You get the picture. There are too many variables to track.

For this reason, we use arrays. For storing 10 ages, we can just use.

```
age=[5,25,45,60,20,23,24,43,34,78];
```

To access the values in Javascript, we use the index of the array. The index of the 1st element is 0, 2nd is 1, 3rd is 2 and so on…. For example,

document.write(age[0]) outputs **5**;

document.write(age[1]) outputs **25**;

document.write(age[5]) outputs **23**.

Example 1 – Creating An Array in JavaScript

Now, let's look at the example below. We create 3 arrays in JavaScript for name, age and state of 5 people. We print these out using array index. And then we add a 6th person using .**push()** feature. Check out the code and output below.

```
<html>
 <head><title>JavaScript Lesson 5 - Arrays</title></head>
<body>
 <link rel="stylesheet" href="samplestyle.css" />


 <button onclick="createarray()">Print Array</button>
<script>

 function createarray()
{
 document.write('<link rel="stylesheet" type="text/css" href="samplestyle.css" />');
 document.write('<br>');

 var nm = ["Jim","Tim","Kim","Bim","Sam"];
 var age=[7,56,40,34,56];
 var state=["Florida","California","Georgia", "Illinois", "Nevada"];
 document.write(nm[0]+' lives in '+state[0]+' state and age is '+age[0]+"<br>");
 document.write(nm[1]+' lives in '+state[1]+' state and age is '+age[1]+"<br>");
 document.write(nm[2]+' lives in '+state[2]+' state and age is '+age[2]+"<br>");
 document.write(nm[3]+' lives in '+state[3]+' state and age is '+age[3]+"<br>");
 document.write(nm[4]+' lives in '+state[4]+' state and age is '+age[4]+"<br>");
 name.push("Yang");//Adding another index to the array
 age.push(20);
 loc.push("California");
 document.write(nm[5]+' lives in '+state[5]+' state and age is '+age[5]+"<br>");



}

</script>


</body>
</html>
```

Output:

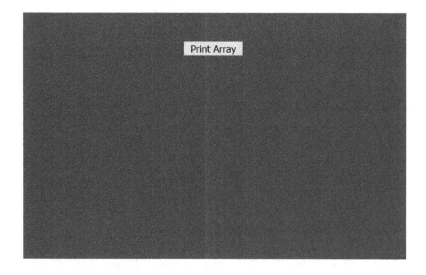

On clicking **Print Array**, we get..

> Jim Lives In Florida State And Age Is 7
> Tim Lives In California State And Age Is 56
> Kim Lives In Georgia State And Age Is 40
> Bim Lives In Illinois State And Age Is 34
> Sam Lives In Nevada State And Age Is 56

Example 2 – Assigning An Array Through A Form

In this example, we input name, age and state through a html form. In Javascript, we assign the form elements to variables.

3 names, ages and state locations are entered via a form and entered into 3 arrays using **document.getElementById**.

The array is printed at the end using **document.write()**.

```html
<html>
<head><title>JavaScript Lesson 5 - Arrays</title></head>
<body>
<link rel="stylesheet" href="samplestyle.css" />
Enter Name1 <input name="name" type="text" id="name0" size="20"><br>
Enter Age1 <input name="age" type="number" id="age0" size="20"><br>
Enter State1 <input name="state" type="text" id="state0" size="20"><br>

Enter Name2 <input name="name" type="text" id="name1" size="20"><br>
Enter Age2 <input name="age" type="number" id="age1" size="20"><br>
Enter State2 <input name="state" type="text" id="state1" size="20"><br>

Enter Name3 <input name="name" type="text" id="name2" size="20"><br>
Enter Age4 <input name="age" type="number" id="age2" size="20"><br>
Enter State4 <input name="state" type="text" id="state2" size="20"><br>
<button onclick="createarray()">Start Program</button>

<script>

function createarray()
{
var nm=[];
var age=[];
var state=[];

nm[0]=document.getElementById("name0").value;
age[0]=document.getElementById("age0").value;
state[0]=document.getElementById("state0").value;
nm[1]=document.getElementById("name1").value;
age[1]=document.getElementById("age1").value;
state[1]=document.getElementById("state1").value;
nm[2]=document.getElementById("name2").value;
age[2]=document.getElementById("age2").value;
state[2]=document.getElementById("state2").value;

document.write('<link rel="stylesheet" type="text/css" href="samplestyle.css" />');
document.write('<br>');
document.write(nm[0] + " is "+age[0]+" years old and lives in "+state[0]+"<br>");
document.write(nm[1] + " is "+age[1]+" years old and lives in "+state[1]+"<br>");
document.write(nm[2] + " is "+age[2]+" years old and lives in "+state[2]+"<br>");

}
```

152

Output:

Enter Name1 Mather
Enter Age1 35
Enter State1 Illinois
Enter Name2 Timmy
Enter Age2 23
Enter State2 Georgia
Enter Name3 Mahama
Enter Age4 67
Enter State4 California
Start Program

On Clicking **Start Program**, we get:

Mather Is 35 Years Old And Lives In Illinois
Timmy Is 23 Years Old And Lives In Georgia
Mahama Is 67 Years Old And Lives In California

Example 3 – Guess World Capitals

In this program, we code a quiz that asks the user the capital of a random country around the world, and checks if the answer is correct.

In the program, the one button runs the **worldquiz()** function. In the function, we declare two arrays. One array contains all the countries around the world; and the other contains all the capitals.

You can get the values for these arrays below:

https://drive.google.com/file/d/1Vbnrllk290oVmh3Vn8Jv2EgFBL1w8vSd/view?usp=sharing

We then chose a random number between 0 and x, x being the length of the array. This random number picks a random country from the array. We do this using **Math.random()** and **Math.floor()**.

We take in a user guess for the capital using **prompt**. We compare the user guess to the actual capital. Then, we send the user a message telling them they're correct or wrong (with the correct capital if they're wrong).

Then, the user has the chance to restart the program with the **Home** button that runs the **redirect()** function. The redirect function runs

'GuessWorldCapitals.html' which is the name of the file. The code and the outputs are shown below.

```html
<html>
<head><title>Guess World Capitals</title>
<link rel="stylesheet" href="styles.css" />
</head>
<body>
<button class="btn a" onclick="worldquiz()">Start Quiz</button>
<script>

function worldquiz()
{

var countries = ["Afghanistan","Albania","Algeria","Andorra","Angola","Antigua and Barbuda","Argentina","Armenia",
var capitals = ["Kabul","Tirana (Tirane)","Algiers","Andorra la Vella","Luanda","Saint John's","Buenos Aires","Yere
var randomcountrynumber = Math.floor(Math.random() * countries.length);
var chosencountry = countries[randomcountrynumber];
var chosencapital = capitals[randomcountrynumber];
var guess = prompt("What is the capital of "+chosencountry+" ?");

if (guess.toUpperCase()==chosencapital.toUpperCase())
{
    document.write("<p>Congratulations. You are correct.</p>");
}else
{
    document.write("<p>Wrong. The capital is "+chosencapital+"</p>");
}

document.write('<link rel="stylesheet" type="text/css" href="styles.css" />');
document.write('<br>');

document.write('<button onClick="redirect()">Home</button>');

}
function redirect()
{
window.location.replace("GuessWorldCapitals.html");
}

</script>
</body>
</html>
```

Output #1:

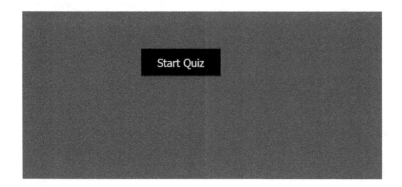

Click **Start Quiz**

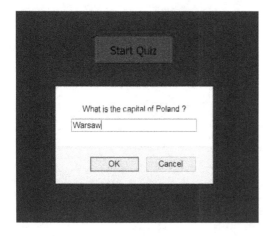

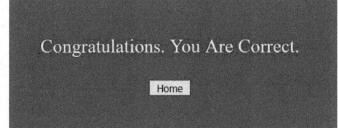

Output #2:

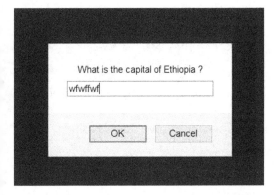

Example 4 – Random Jokes

This program prints a random joke out a random joke picked from a list of jokes. The one button runs the **writejoke()** function. In the function, we declare an array that contains all the jokes.

You can get the values for the array below:

https://drive.google.com/file/d/1xDN9dt2Gvj-mdPmi5ATCnP1tvOZtZt25/view?usp=sharing

We then chose a random number between 0 and x, x is the length of the array. This random number picks a random country. We do this using **Math.random()** and **Math.floor()**.

We then print out the joke using the **document.write()** function.

Then, the user has the chance to restart the program with the **Home** button that runs the **redirect()** function.

```html
<html>
<head><title>Random Duck Jokes</title>
<link rel="stylesheet" href="samplestyle.css" />
</head>
<body>
<button class="btn a" onclick="writejoke()">Get A Duck Joke</button>
<script>
var duckjokes = [
"Why did the duck cross the road?                        It was the chicken's day off",
"Why did the duck detective get promoted?          He quacked the case",
"Why did the tiger cross the road?                   To eat the duck and the hen",
"What did the duck do when he saw the clown?         He started quacking up",
"Why is the duck always standing straight?            To hide his butt-quack",
"Which is the heaviest bird?                    The crane",
"Why did the duck go to prison?                    He became a quackpot.",
"Why did the bee do his own haircuts?              He did buzzcuts",
"Why did the duck lose the race?              Because he was a lame duck",
"What happened after the duck got injured?        He went to a ducktor!",
"Where did the duck eat breakfast?               Quacker barrel",
"Why did the hen keep its nest warm?         Because it was eggstremely cold outside",
"Why did the duck not like the soup?            Because it had no quackers!",
"Why were the two ducks always together?        They were stuck together with duck-tape",
"Why do swans avoid the stock market?          Because they're afraid of the black-swan",
"How do ducks know if it's about to rain?           They checked the feather-forecast",
"What did the duck do on July 4th?            It burst quackers",
]
function writejoke()
{
var chosenjoke = duckjokes[Math.floor(Math.random() * duckjokes.length)];

document.write(chosenjoke);
document.write('<link rel="stylesheet" type="text/css" href="samplestyle.css" />');
document.write('<br>');
document.write('<button onClick="redirect()">Home</button>');
}
function redirect()
{
window.location.replace("RandomJoke.html");
}
</script>

</body>
</html>
```

159

Output #1:

Where Did The Duck Eat Breakfast? Quacker Barrel
Home

Output #2:

Why Did The Hen Keep Its Nest Warm? Because It Was Eggstremely Cold Outside

Home

Example 5 – Animal Hangman

This program codes a fun game of animal hangman. The button in the program below starts the function **animalhangman()**. In the function, we first declare an array that contains all the animals. Then, we pick a random animal using Math.random() and Math.floor().

We create a variable that stores the answer (**answerArray**). It stores the user answer. It is initialized to underscores (_) with the same length as the original animal.

The variable **remletters** is the number of remaining letters to be guessed. A while loop is created to accept user guesses as long as **remletters>0**.

Using prompt, we accept a single letter input from the user. If there is more than one letter input, we set an error message and ask the user to enter only one letter. Once the user enters a letter, we enter a loop that checks each letter of the random animal against the user letter. Each time there is a match, we subtract **remletters** by 1 and update the relevant part of **answerArray** with the matched letters. At the end of the while loop, the user has guessed the animal, and we print out a congratulatory note with the name of the animal.

At any point within the while loop, if the user doesn't enter a letter and tries to proceed, we exit the program loop and print out the animal name.

At the end of the game, the user has the option to restart the program using the **Home** button. Here's the code below with some examples.

```html
<html>
<head>
 <title>Animal Hangman</title>
 <link rel="stylesheet" href="samplestyle.css" />
</head>
<body>
<button class="btn" onclick="animalhangmman()">Start Animal Hangman</button>

<script>
function animalhangmman()
{
 // Create an array of animals
 var animals = [
 "tiger",
 "lion",
 "monkey",
 "kangaroo",
 "racoon",
 "flamingo",
 "elephant",
 "porcupine"
 ];
 var chosenanimal = animals[Math.floor(Math.random() * animals.length)];
 var answerArray = [];
 for (var i = 0; i < chosenanimal.length; i++) {
 answerArray[i] = "_";
 }
```

```
var remletters = chosenanimal.length;
while (remletters > 0)
{
alert(answerArray.join(" "));
var guess = prompt("Guess a letter, or click Cancel to stop playing.");
if (guess == null)
{
// Exit the game loop
break;
}
else if (guess.length !== 1)
{
alert("Please enter a single letter.");
}
else
{
// Update the game state with the guess
for (var j = 0; j < chosenanimal.length; j++)
{
if (chosenanimal[j] === guess)
{
answerArray[j] = guess;
remletters=remletters-1;
}
}
} // The end of the game loop
}
// Show the answer and congratulate the player
alert(answerArray.join(" "));
alert("Good job! The answer was " + chosenanimal);
}
</script>
</body>
</html>
```

Output #1

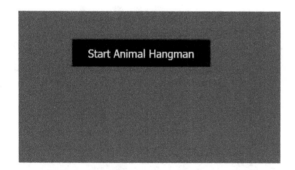

Below is the starting point showing the length of the answer.

164

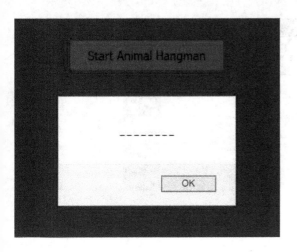

Guess the first letter. The user enters 't'

There is no 't'. So we try again.

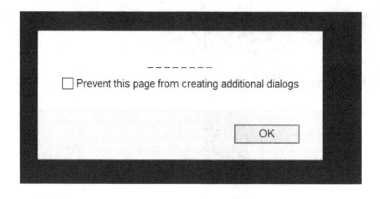

The user enters 'k'

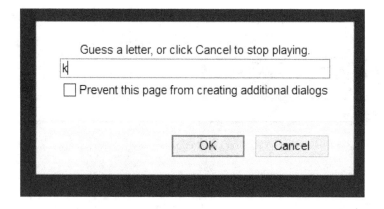

No 'k' in the answer. Still no correct guess.

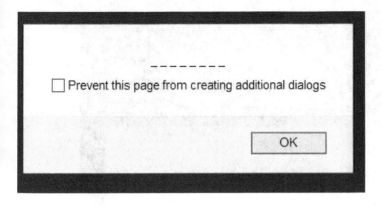

Now, the user enters 'o'

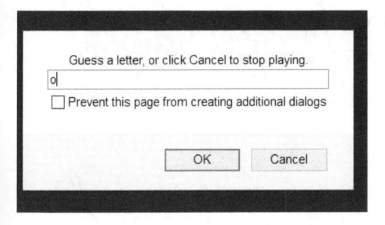

Finally, the user guesses correct. The word ends with 'o' and we see that in

the updated answer.

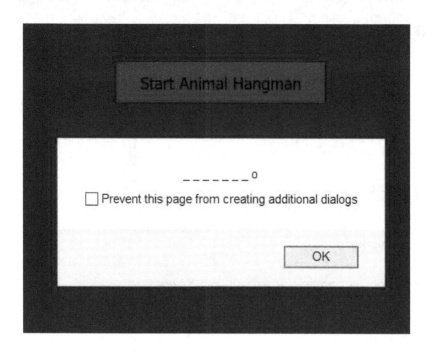

So, after a few more guesses of this, we arrive at answer below. Just one more guess.

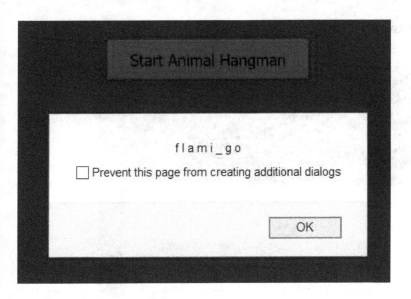

The user guesses 'n'.

And that is correct. The entire word is flamingo.

And, the program displays the correct answer below.

Start Animal Hangman

Good job! The answer was flamingo

☐ Prevent this page from creating additional dialogs

OK

1. Create a resume that takes in multiple candidates through a form and stores them in separate arrays. One array for names, one for cities, one for university and one for GPA. Print out all the names that are in a particular city.

2. Write a program that is a quiz about US Presidents. Create an array of all US Presidents. Create another array that has a well-known fact about each US President. Have a program that randomly chooses a fact to present to the user; and the user can guess who that is.

3. Write a program that lists all the cars that the dealership has in an array. Another corresponding array has all the prices of those cars; and a third has the year of manufacture in a year. The program takes in a model year from the user and prints all the cars and prices of cars newer than that year.

4. Write a program that plays a game of sports hangman. Pick a sport; and pick your 20 favourite players in that sport. Put the players in an array of size 20 and have the user guess the letters as in a game of hangman.

Objects

An object in programming is a collection of properties with values for each property. These properties need not be the same variable types. For example, we can have an object with both string and numerical properties.

Example 1

In the example below, we create an object for a car. It has 4 different properties, one for name, one for model, one for price, one for license plate. These are accepted through user input via forms.

They are accepted as input in the **entercar()** function and then assigned to an object in printcars() function. In the **printcars()** functions, the user inputs via forms are assigned to 4 separate variables.

These variables are assigned to the object car as shown below. The property and value are separated from one another using: and the different property/values are separated using a comma(,)

In the below example, type, model, license and price are properties; while

carname, carmodel, carnumber and **carprice** are the values of the respective

properties. The 4 values below are the ones that are from the user form.

```
var car={type:carname,model:carmodel,license:carnumber,price:carprice};
```

And to access the object values, we use the dot(.) operator before the

property. For example, **car.type** will give you the value assigned to property

'type' of object **'car'**.

And thus, we print out car type and price by accessing the object property

value.

The code is available below with outputs.

```html
<html>
<head><title>Car Check</title></head>
<link rel="stylesheet" href="samplestyle.css" />
<body>
<button class="btn" onclick="entercar()">Start Car</button>
<script>
function entercar()
{
document.write("Car Name: ");
document.write('<input name="name" type="text" id="carname" size="20"><br>');
document.write("Car Model: ");
document.write('<input name="name" type="text" id="carmodel" size="20"><br>');
document.write("License Plate: ");
document.write('<input name="name" type="text" id="carnumber" size="20"><br>');
document.write("Car price: ");
document.write('<input name="name" type="number" id="carprice" size="20"><br>');
document.write('<link rel="stylesheet" type="text/css" href="styles.css" />');
document.write('<br>');
document.write('<button class="btn a" onclick="printcars()">Check</button><br>');
document.write('<link rel="stylesheet" type="text/css" href="samplestyle.css" />');
document.write('<br>');
}
function printcars()
{
var carname=document.getElementById("carname").value;
var carmodel=document.getElementById("carmodel").value;
var carnumber=document.getElementById("carnumber").value;
var carprice=document.getElementById("carprice").value;
var car={type:carname,model:carmodel,license:carnumber,price:carprice};
document.write("Type of car = "+car.type+"<br>");
document.write("Price of car = "+car.price)+"<br>";
}

function redirect()
{
window.location.replace("ObjectsCars.html");
}
</script>
</body>
</html>
```

175

Output 1:

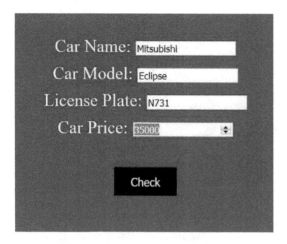

After clicking **Check** button, we get:

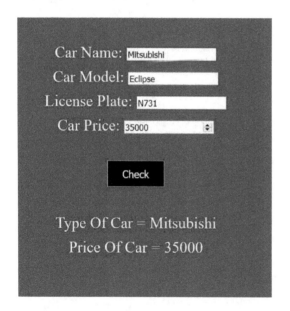

Example 2

In the below example, we simulate a game of dice between 6 players.

Basically, a game of dice is played 10 times; and points are added to the players depending on where the dice falls between 1-6. For example, if it falls on 1, a point is added to Player 1. If it falls on 2, a point is added to Player 2 and so on. The value of the dice is simulated between 1 and 6 using **Math.Random()** function.

At the start of the program, an object **gameplayer** is declared. The property is the name of the player, and the value is the number of points obtained.

In the function **dicegame()**, there is a **FOR** loop that runs **gamecalc()** 10 times. In gamecalc() a random number between 1 and 6 is chosen, which simulates the rolling of the dice. Depending on what value the dice falls on, a player's property value is increased by 10.

At the end of the **FOR** loop, we print out the points obtained by each player below.

The code is below with a sample output.

```html
<html>
<head><title>Game Score Keeper</title></head>
<link rel="stylesheet" href="samplestyle.css" />
<body>
<button class="btn" onclick="dicegame()">Start Playing</button>

<script>
var gameplayers={"Adam": 0,"Bob":7,"Carol":0,"Steve":4,"Mark":2,"Tim":0,};

function dicegame()
{

for (i=0;i<10;i++)
{
gamecalc();
}
document.write("<br>");
document.write("Adam scored "+gameplayers["Adam"]+ " points.<br>");
document.write("Bob scored "+gameplayers["Bob"]+ " points.<br>");
document.write("Carol scored "+gameplayers["Carol"]+ " points.<br>");
document.write("Steve scored "+gameplayers["Steve"]+ " points.<br>");
document.write("Mark scored "+gameplayers["Mark"]+ " points.<br>");
document.write("Tim scored "+gameplayers["Tim"]+ " points.<br>");


document.write('<link rel="stylesheet" type="text/css" href="samplestyle.css" />');
document.write('<br>');

document.write('<button class="btn a" onclick="dicegame()">Check</button><br>');

}
```

```javascript
function gamecalc()
{
score=Math.floor((Math.random() * 6) + 1);

if(score==1)
{
gameplayers["Abhishek"]=gameplayers["Abhishek"]+10;
document.write("Abhishek won 10 points.<br>");
}
if(score==2)
{
gameplayers["Bob"]=gameplayers["Bob"]+10;
document.write("Bob won 10 points.<br>");
}
if(score==3)
{
gameplayers["Carol"]=gameplayers["Carol"]+10;
document.write("Carol won 10 points.<br>");
}
if(score==4)
{
gameplayers["Steve"]=gameplayers["Steve"]+10;
document.write("Steve won 10 points.<br>");
}
if(score==5)
{
gameplayers["Mark"]=gameplayers["Mark"]+10;
document.write("Mark won 10 points.<br>");
}
if(score==6)
{
gameplayers["Tim"]=gameplayers["Tim"]+10;
document.write("Tim won 10 points.<br>");
}
}
function redirect()
{
window.location.replace("ObjectsCars.html");
}

</script>
</body>
</html>
```

Output:

The top 10 lines of the output show who won the dice game in the 10

iterations of the loop.

The bottom 6 lines show the final scores obtained by the players.

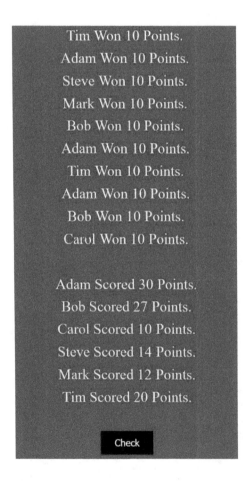

Practice Problems

1. Write a program that creates an object for a restaurant menu. The properties are the dish name, time to cook and price of dish. And then access the object values to print out all the dishes that cost below $20 and cook below 20 minutes.

2. Write a program that simulates shooting practice for a basketball game. The name of the player is the property and the points scored is the value assigned to the property. The program checks the name of the player and whether the shot is outside the 3-point circle. Based on the answer, it adds 2 or 3 points to the relevant player.

Creating a Canvas

What is a Canvas?

A canvas is a html element allows that allows the user to draw graphics, shapes, images and run animations using JavaScript. It is a rectangular area on the html page, the size of which we can define.

Canvas Example

The size of a canvas is defined in the unit of pixels. A pixel is the smallest unit of illumination on a computer screen. The most used computer size is 1366 pixels width by 768 pixels height.

Below is the sample canvas, which has a width of 500 pixels and height of 500 pixels. It has a visible border of 2 pixels around the canvas.

```
<html>
<head><title>Sample Canvas</title>
</head>
<body>
<canvas id="myCanvas" width="500" height="500" style="border:2px solid"></canvas><br>
<script>

</script>
</body>
</html>
```

Output:

Drawing (with measurements):

Below is the drawing with the canvas size relative to the regular computer monitor screen. The green measurements are the size of the computer screen, and the black measurements are the size of the canvas. One can only draw on the canvas and not on the rest of the screen.

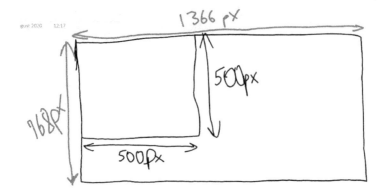

Creating a Circle on the Canvas

A circle in JavaScript is created using 5 steps. That's what we do in the code below.

The first step is to convert the html element to a JavaScript variable using document.getElementByID. Then it is converted to a 2D drawing element variable using getContext("2d"). In the below example, variable c2x is the drawing element.

We can start any drawing in JavaScript with **beginPath()** and then clear the canvas using **clearRect**. Here's how **clearRect** works, as in the below example:

clearRect(a,b,c,d) means that the top left corner of the rectangle starts at an x-coordinate of **a** and y-cooridnate of **b**; it has a width of **c** and a height of **d**.

So, we start at (a,b), and clear a canvas of width c and height d. In the

example below, we start at (0,0), and clear the entire canvas of width 500

pixels and height 500 pixels. This makes the entire canvas blanks and ready to

draw.

Next, we draw the circle using the arc function. So, let's see how that works:

arc(a,b,c,d,e) is how we draw the circle. (a,b) is the center of the circle; a

being the x-coordinate and b being the y-coordinate. c is the radius of the

circle. d is the starting part of the arc of the circle. e is the ending part of the

arc.

d and e are measured in radians. For a full circle, d and e would be 0 and 2π

respectively. For a half-circle d and e would be between 0 and π.

In the below example, Circle 1 center is at (50,50) and has a radius of 20

pixels. Circle 2 is at a center point of (250,250) and has a larger radius of 70.

Circle 3 is actually a semi-circle as it goes from 0 to π radians. It is closer to

the bottom right hand corner at (350,350) and has a radius of 50 pixels.

In the final step we draw the circles using stroke(). If we want to fill the

circles, we do so using fill(). And we can change the color using fillStyle().

```html
<html>
<head><title>Sample Canvas</title>
</head>
<body>
<canvas id="acanvas" width="500" height="500" style="border:2px solid"></canvas><br>
<button class="btn a" onclick="drawcircle()">Draw Circle</button>

<script>
function drawcircle()
{
var i = document.getElementById("acanvas");
var c2x = i.getContext("2d");

//Circe1
c2x.beginPath();
c2x.clearRect(0, 0, 500, 500);
c2x.arc(50,50,20,0,2*Math.PI);
c2x.fillStyle = "red";
c2x.stroke();
c2x.fill();

//Circle2
c2x.beginPath();
c2x.arc(250,250,70,0,2*Math.PI);
c2x.fillStyle = "blue";
c2x.stroke();
c2x.fill();

//Circle3
c2x.beginPath();
c2x.arc(350,350,50,0,1*Math.PI);
c2x.fillStyle = "green";
c2x.stroke();
c2x.fill();
}

</script>
</body>
</html>
```

186

Output:

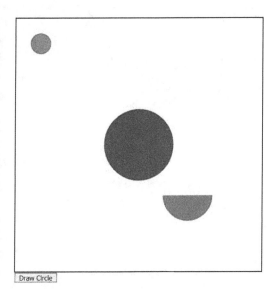

Draw Circle

Drawing (Measurements):

Here's Circle 2 (blue circle) measuring using the canvas co-ordinates, just to show an example.

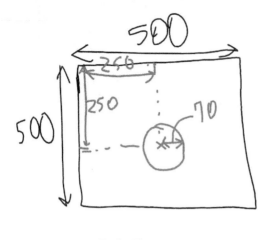

Circle #2

Creating a Rectangle on the Canvas

The drawing of a rectangle begins the same way as of a circle; with the canvas and 2D context variables. Again, we use **beginPath()** and **clearRect()** to start the process. Then we use a function known as **fillRect()** which is shown below:

fillRect(a,b,c,d) means that the top left corner of the rectangle starts at an x-coordinate of **a** and y-cooridnate of **b**; it has a width of **c** and a height of **d**. So, we start at **(a,b)**, and clear a canvas of width c and height d. In the example below, we start at **(0,0)**, and creates a rectangle of width 50 pixels and height 100 pixels. It is a red triangle (since fillRect is red).

188

There is a second **fillRect()** which creates a square of width 75 pixels (as both width and height are set to the same value of 75). The top left corner of the square starts at **(150,150)**.

In both cases, fillRect() automatically draws and fills the rectangle with the assigned color.

```
<html>
<head><title>Sample Canvas</title>
</head>
<body>
<canvas id="acanvas" width="500" height="500" style="border:2px solid"></canvas><br>
<button class="btn a" onclick="drawsquare()">Draw Square</button>

<script>
function drawsquare()
{
var i = document.getElementById("acanvas");
var c2x = i.getContext("2d");

//Rectangle 1
c2x.beginPath();
c2x.fillStyle = "red";
c2x.clearRect(0, 0, 500, 500);
c2x.fillRect(0, 0, 50, 100);

//Square 1
c2x.beginPath();
c2x.fillStyle = "blue";
c2x.fillRect(150, 150, 75, 75);

}

</script>
</body>
</html>
```

Output:

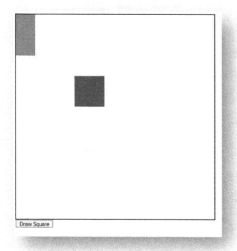

Drawing (Rectangle 2):

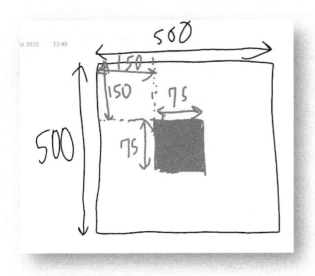

Creating a Smiley Face

In the below example, we use our knowledge of circles and semi-circles to create a smiley face.

First, we do a yellow circle of 75 pixel radius in the center of the screen, which is the face. We then draw 2 small black circles of 10 pixels each which serve as the eyes.

And finally, we do a semi-circle filled with black color of radius 30 pixels. This is the smile.

Pretty cute, huh? You can get creative and make any face you want.

```
<html>
<head><title>Smiley Face</title>
</head>
<body>
<canvas id="acanvas" width="500" height="500" style="border:2px solid"></canvas><br>
<button class="btn a" onclick="drawsquare()">Draw Square</button>

<script>
function drawsquare()
{
var i = document.getElementById("acanvas");
var c2x = i.getContext("2d");

//Yellow Face
c2x.beginPath();
c2x.clearRect(0, 0, 500, 500);
c2x.arc(250,250,75,0,2*Math.PI);
c2x.fillStyle = "yellow";
c2x.stroke();
c2x.fill();

//Black Eyes
c2x.beginPath();
c2x.arc(225,225,10,0,2*Math.PI);
c2x.fillStyle = "black";
c2x.stroke();
c2x.fill();

c2x.beginPath();
c2x.arc(275,225,10,0,2*Math.PI);
c2x.fillStyle = "black";
c2x.stroke();
c2x.fill();

//Black Smile

c2x.beginPath();
c2x.arc(250,275,30,0,1*Math.PI);
c2x.fillStyle = "black";
c2x.stroke();
c2x.fill();

}
```

192

Output:

Draw Square

Practice Problems

1. Create a canvas of 700 pixels by 500 pixels. Draw 4 circles on the 4 different corners of the canvas. And then draw a 5th circle right on the centre of the canvas. All circles are of different colors. This is a good canvas to get you comfortable with positioning shapes on the screen.

2. Create a canvas of 600 pixels by 600 pixels. Draw different emoticons on the screen. Draw a smiley face at the center of the canvas. Then, do a frowny face right on top of it. Third, do a scared emoticon (with closed eyes and straight mouth) at the right of center. And finally, do an emoticon of your choice to the left.

3. Create a canvas of 600 pixels by 600 pixels. Draw a square right at the center of side 100 pixels. Then draw a second square of 80 pixels. Third, draw a square of 60 pixels…. And so on, tell it can't get any smaller. This is an example of concentric squares. (Hint: A square is just a rectangle with all equal sides).

Timer and Animations

What is a Timer?

A timer in Javascript is used to time Javascript code. It allows the user to execute different portions of the code at different time intervals.

setTimeOut() and **setTimeInterval()** functions are used to set the timer. **setTimeOut()** allows a fixed break before executing a code; **settimeinterval()** allows the code to be executed multiple times with a fixed interval between each execution. For example:

setTimeOut(a, 1000) executes the function **a** after **1000 ms (1 second).**

setTimeInterval(a, 1000) keeps executing the function with a break of **1000 ms (1 second)** between runs.

These functions are the key to running JavaScript animations.

Timer Example

In our code, we only use the **setInterval()** function. In the example below, we have two buttons that run two separate functions.

The first function **writename()** prints the name "Bob" on the screen every 2500 ms (or 2.5 seconds). The function **fname()** is run using **setinterval(fname, 2500)** and write the name "Bob".

The second function runs the function **setcount()** prints numbers starting from 1 and increments it by 1 each time with a break of 500 ms (0.5 seconds). So, it prints 1,2,3,4 and so on with a break of 0.5 seconds between each print.

```
<html>
<head><title>Counting Timer</title>
</head>
<body>
<link rel="stylesheet" href="samplestyle.css" />
<button class="btn a" onclick="setcount()">Count</button>
<button class="btn a" onclick="writename()">Write Name</button>

<script>
function writename()
{
var name="Bob";
setInterval(fname, 2500);
function fname()
{
  document.write('<link rel="stylesheet" type="text/css" href="samplestyle.css" />');
  document.write(name);
  document.write("<br>");
}
}

function setcount()
{
count=0;
setInterval(timeUp, 500);
function timeUp()
{
  document.write('<link rel="stylesheet" type="text/css" href="samplestyle.css" />');
  count=count+1;
  document.write(count);
  document.write("<br>");

}
}
</script>
</body>
</html>
```

Output 1:

On clicking **Count**,

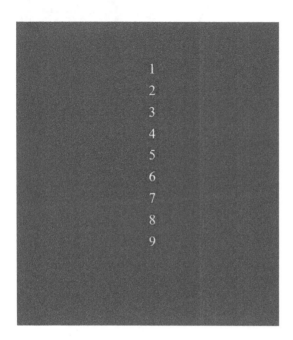

Output #2

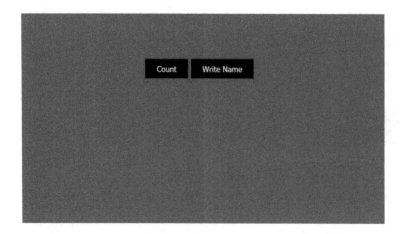

On clicking **Count**

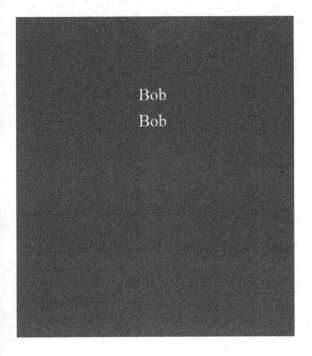

Growing Square

We use the **setInterval** and **fillRect** functions to write a program that expands a square. A button when clicked runs the growing square function. In the growing square functions, we do a **setinterval** where we run the function **frame()** every 10 ms (0.01 seconds). We declare a variable size to 10 pixels. **Size** contains the length of the square.

In the function frame, we first clear the entire canvas using **clearRect().** Then we draw a rectangle starting at (0,0) of length 'size'. **Size** is increased by 5 every time the function is executed. Once size is greater than the 500, it is set back to 10. This ensures that once the square is larger than the canvas, it restarts growing from a small size.

```
<html>
<head><title>Growing Square</title>
</head>
<body>
<canvas id="myCanvas" width="500" height="500" style="border:2px solid"></canvas><br>
<button class="btn a" onclick="growingsquare()">Square</button>
<script>
function growingsquare()
{
var i = document.getElementById("myCanvas");
var c2x = i.getContext("2d");
setInterval(frame, 10);
size=10;
function frame()
{
  if (size>500)
  {
  size=0;
  }
  c2x.clearRect(0, 0, 500, 500);
  c2x.fillRect(0, 0, size, size);
  size=size+5;
}
}
</script>
</body>
</html>
```

Output:

Square

Drawing (Square grows)

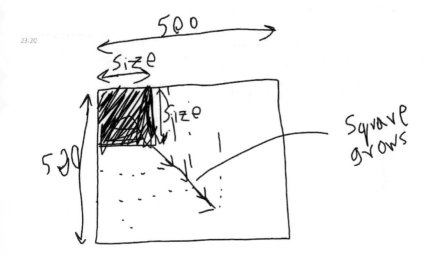

Growing Circle

We use the **setInterval** and **arc** functions to write a program that expands a circle. A button when clicked runs the growing square function. In the growing square functions, we do a **setinterval** where we run the function **frame()** every 50 ms (0.05 seconds). We declare a variable size to 10 pixels. **Size** contains the radius of the circle.

In the function frame, we first clear the entire canvas using **clearRect()**. Then we draw a circle starting at the center of (250,250) of radius 'size'. **Size** is increased by 5 every time the loop is executed. Once size is greater than the

203

350, it is set back to 10. This ensures that once the circle is larger than the

canvas, it restarts growing from a small size.

```
<html>
<head><title>Growing Circle</title>
</head>
<body>
<canvas id="myCanvas" width="500" height="500" style="border:2px solid"></canvas><br>
<button class="btn a" onclick="growingcircle()">Circle</button>
<script>
function growingcircle()
{
var c = document.getElementById("myCanvas");
var ctx = c.getContext("2d");
setInterval(frame, 50);
size=10;
function frame()
{
//Circle
if (size>350)
{
size=10;
}
ctx.beginPath();
ctx.clearRect(0, 0, 500, 500);
ctx.arc(250,250,size,0,2*Math.PI);
ctx.fillStyle = "blue";
ctx.stroke();
ctx.fill();
size=size+5;
}
}
</script>
</body>
</html>
```

Output:

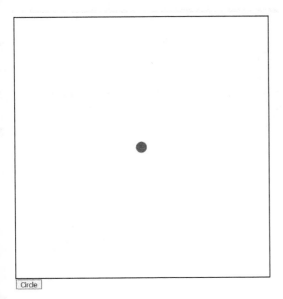

Circle

Circle

Drawing (Circle)

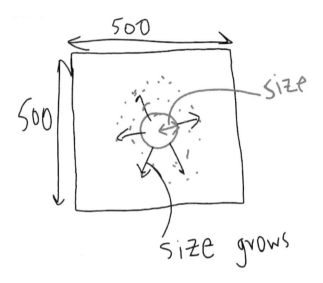

Growing Radial Circle

A radial circle is very similar to a circle. A radial circle controls the color of the circle, the background and can also add an extra color to the border between the circle and the background. In the below example, we create a radial circle of color red with a blue background. And there is a yellow border to the red ball, which acts like an annulus.

In the below example, **createRadialGradient()** is used to create the circle. This is how it works.

createRadialGradiant(a,b,c,d,e,f) creates an inner circle with **center (a,b)** with radius **c**. The second circle creates a circle with **center (d,e)** with radius **f**. If we want an annular circle then we should have them at same center i.e. **(a,b) = (d,e).**

In the below example, we have an inner circle and outer circle at the center of the canvas **(250,250)**. The radius of the outer circle is always **20** pixels more than the inner circle.

The inner circle color is set to red using **addColorStop(0,"red")** and the the background is set to blue using **addColorStop(1,"blue")**. Finally, the outer circle color is set to yellow using **addColorStop(0.5,"yellow")**.

The radial circle keeps growing by 5 pixels every 50 ms (0.5 seconds). If the size of the circle exceeds the canvas, it is set back to 10 pixels.

```
<html>
<head><title>Growing Circle</title>
</head>
<body>
<canvas id="mCanvas" width="500" height="500" style="border:2px solid"></canvas><br>
<button class="btn a" onclick="growingcircle()">Circle</button>
<script>
function growingcircle()
{
var c = document.getElementById("mCanvas");
var c2x = c.getContext("2d");
setInterval(frame, 50);
size=10;
function frame()
{
//Circle
if (size>350)
{
size=10;
}
c2x.beginPath();
var grd = c2x.createRadialGradient(250, 250, size, 250, 250, size+20);
grd.addColorStop(0, "red");
grd.addColorStop(0.5, "yellow");
grd.addColorStop(1, "blue");

// Fill with gradient
c2x.fillStyle = grd;
c2x.fillRect(0, 0, 500, 500);
c2x.stroke();
c2x.fill();
size=size+5;
}
}
</script>
</body>
</html>
```

Output:

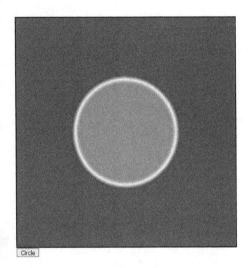

Circle

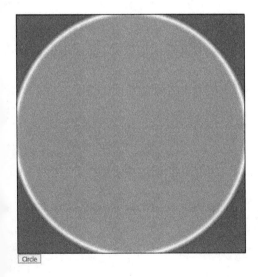

Circle

Drawing:

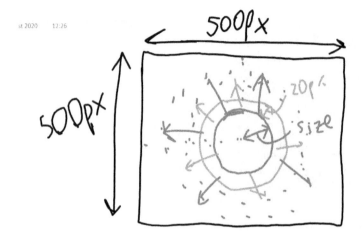

Moving Ball in Different Directions

In the below example, we use the timer and ball functions to move the ball in 4 different directions using 4 buttons. Each button runs the function that moves the ball in a particular direction.

For example, if we press down, it moves the ball down using the **MoveDown()** function. Once the ball reaches the bottom of the canvas, it restarts from the top again.

In each of the functions, we set a position variable to indicate starting point of the ball. In MoveUp() and MoveDown() we set the y position to 500 and 0 respectively. Using the setInterval function we increase/decrease the position

variable by 5 pixels to move the ball every 50 ms (0.05 seconds). And, we use

the IF function to check if the ball has reached the end of the canvas, and set

it back to the original function.

```html
<html>
<head><title>Growing Circle</title>
</head>
<body>
<canvas id="myCanvas" width="500" height="500" style="border:2px solid"></canvas><br>
<button class="btn a" onclick="MoveDown()">Down</button>
<button class="btn a" onclick="MoveUp()">Up</button>
<button class="btn a" onclick="MoveRight()">Right</button>
<button class="btn a" onclick="MoveLeft()">Left</button>

<script>
function MoveDown()
{
var c = document.getElementById("myCanvas");
var ctx = c.getContext("2d");
setInterval(frame, 50);
locy=10;
function frame()
{
//Circle
if (locy>500)
{
locy=10;
}
ctx.beginPath();
ctx.clearRect(0, 0, 500, 500);
ctx.arc(250,locy,30,0,2*Math.PI);
ctx.fillStyle = "blue";
ctx.stroke();
ctx.fill();
locy=locy+5;
}
}
```

```
function MoveUp()
{
var c = document.getElementById("myCanvas");
var ctx = c.getContext("2d");
setInterval(frame, 50);
locy=500;
function frame()
{
//Circle
if (locy<0)
{
locy=500;
}
ctx.beginPath();
ctx.clearRect(0, 0, 500, 500);
ctx.arc(250,locy,30,0,2*Math.PI);
ctx.fillStyle = "blue";
ctx.stroke();
ctx.fill();
locy=locy-5;
}
}
function MoveRight()
{
var c = document.getElementById("myCanvas");
var ctx = c.getContext("2d");
setInterval(frame, 50);
locx=10;
function frame()
{
//Circle
if (locx>500)
{
locx=10;
}
ctx.beginPath();
ctx.clearRect(0, 0, 500, 500);
ctx.arc(locx,250,30,0,2*Math.PI);
ctx.fillStyle = "blue";
ctx.stroke();
ctx.fill();
locx=locx+5;
}
}
```

```
function MoveLeft()
{
var c = document.getElementById("myCanvas");
var ctx = c.getContext("2d");
setInterval(frame, 50);
locx=500;
function frame()
{
//Circle
if (locx<0)
{
locx=500;
}
ctx.beginPath();
ctx.clearRect(0, 0, 500, 500);
ctx.arc(locx,250,30,0,2*Math.PI);
ctx.fillStyle = "blue";
ctx.stroke();
ctx.fill();
locx=locx-5;
}
}
</script>
</body>
</html>
```

Output #1: Move Down

Position 1

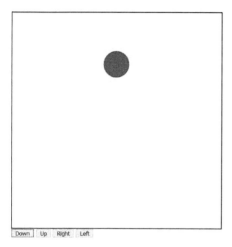

Position 2

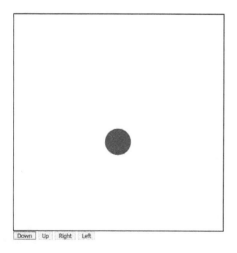

Output #2: Move Left

Position 1

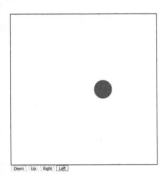

Position 2

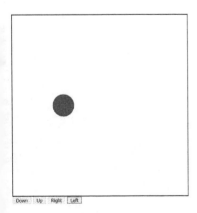

Drawing (Move Down)

As we can see below, locy starts at 10 and keeps increasing to make it move down in the animation.

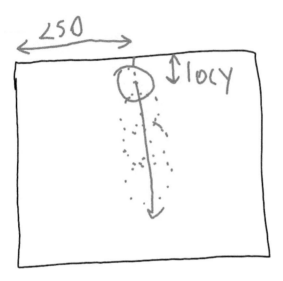

Bouncing Ball

In this example, we move the ball towards the edge of the canvas and the ball bounces back when it hits the canvas.

This is done by modifying the equation that determines the x location and y location of the ball.

Firstly, in this case, we move the ball in both x and y locations at the same time. So, we have two separate variables, **locationx** and **locationy**. There are another 2 variables, that determine the direction in which the ball moves; **snx** and **sny**. If snx is positive, it moves to the right. If snx is negative, it moves to the left. Thus, the equations for locationx and locationy are:

locationx=locationx+snx*5

locationy=locationy+sny*5

So, we move the ball 5 pixels through x (either left or right) and 5 pixels through y (either up or down)

If the ball reaches the side edge of the canvas (**locationy=500** or **locationx =0**), then we change direction of x motion (**snx=snx*-1**).

And, if the ball reaches the upper/lower edge of the canvas (**locationy=500** or

locationy=0) then we change the direction of y-motion (**sny=sny*-1**).

This change of direction creates the bounce that we see on the screen.

```html
<html>
<head><title>Bouncing Ball</title>
</head>
<body>
<canvas id="myCanvas" width="500" height="500" style="border:2px solid"></canvas><br>
<button class="btn a" onclick="bouncingball()">Bounce Ball</button>
<script>
function bouncingball()
{
var c = document.getElementById("myCanvas");
var ctx = c.getContext("2d");
var snx=1;
var sny=1;
setInterval(frame, 10);
locationx=Math.random()*350;
locationy=Math.random()*350;
```

```javascript
function frame()
{
//Circle
ctx.beginPath();
ctx.clearRect(0, 0, 500, 500);
ctx.arc(locationx,locationy,20,0,2*Math.PI);
ctx.fillStyle = "red";
ctx.stroke();
ctx.fill();
if (locationx>=500)
    {
        snx=snx*-1;
    }
if (locationx<=0)
    {
        snx=snx*-1;
    }
if (locationy>=500)
    {
        sny=sny*-1;
    }
if (locationy<=0)
    {
        sny=sny*-1;
    }
locationx=locationx+snx*5;
locationy=locationy+sny*5;
}
}
</script>
</body>
</html>
```

Output

Bounce Ball

Bounce Ball

220

Drawing (Bounce Bottom Wall)

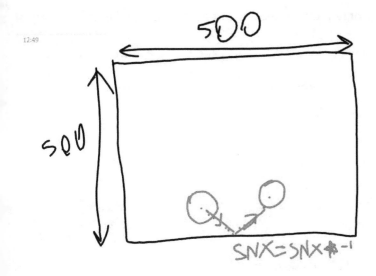

Drawing (Bounce Right Wall)

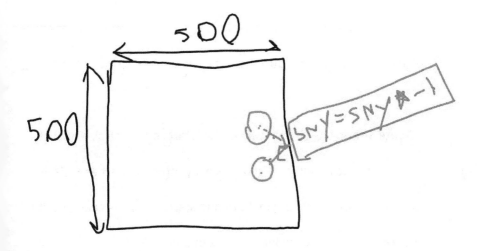

Practice Problems

1. Write a program that accepts a number as input and prints a multiple of that number every 0.5 seconds. For example, if we accept 6 as input; we should print out:

   6

   12

   18

   24...

   And so on, every 0.5 seconds.

2. Modify the **growing square** program so it grows from the centre of the canvas instead of from one corner.

   Hint: You need to add variables for the first 2 co-ordinates of the fillRect function and reduce them by 5 each time to move the corner up and left.

3. Create a shrinking circle problem that starts off at the size of canvas and shrinks to a radius of 5 pixels slowly. When it reaches 5 pixels size, it restarts at the original size and starts shrinking again. So, it's the reverse of our Growing Circle example.

4. Create 2 balls that start at random positions on the canvas; and move in random directions. They bounce off the wall; and if they touch each other, they change directions. (Hint: Create a 2nd ball in the Bouncing Ball program, and then add in a check for the distance between the two balls. If the distance between the two balls is small, change direction of both balls).

KeyPress and Mouse Click Event

What does a KeyPress Element Do?

A KeyPress element detects when a certain event happens on the keyboard. The action of typing a key is called an event.

A KeyPress Element is part of jQuery. jQuery is a JavaScript library used to handle events, animations etc. Below is a simple example of a keypress element.

KeyPress Example 1

Before we start the program, we upload the jQuery library on to the program using below code:

```
<script src="https://code.jquery.com/jquery-2.1.0.js"></script>
```

In Javascript, we create a variable called **keyc** which contains all the keycodes. The keycodes are numbers assigned to every event that occurs when we type on the keyboard. For example, 32 is the keycode for the event of pressing the spacebar. To get a list of all the event keycodes, we can check them on the link below:

https://keycode.info/

We include only 8 keycodes shown in the program; as this is just a test program. Feel free to include more if you want to. Then we have the below code that runs the function **press(event)** when a key is pressed.

$("body").keydown(press)

Inside the function, we use **keyc[event.keycode]** to access the event that happened when we pressed the button. See some examples below for the output.

```
<html>
<head>
  <title>Keyboard input</title>
</head>
<body>
  <script src="https://code.jquery.com/jquery-2.1.0.js"></script>
<script>
var keyc = {
  16: "shift",
  27: "escape",
  32: "space",
  37: "left",
  38: "up",
  39: "right",
  40: "down",
  46: "delete"
};
$("body").keydown(press);
function press(event)
{
document.write("You just pressed the key: "+keyc[event.keyCode]);
}

</script>
</body>
</html>
```

Output:

You just pressed the key: right

You just pressed the key: space

KeyPress Example 2

In the below program, we create 5 different functions that places a small ball

at 5 different parts of the canvas; based on which key is pressed on the

keyboard. If the user presses "space" the program runs **centerballposition()**

which places the ball in the center of the canvas.

If the user presses "right" the program runs **rightballposition()** which places

the ball in the top right corner of the canvas.

227

If the user presses "left" the program runs **leftballposition()** which places the ball in the left top corner of the canvas.

If the user presses "down" the program runs **downballposition()** which places the ball in the bottom right corner of the canvas.

If the user presses "escape" the program runs **downleftballposition()** which places the ball in the bottom left corner of the canvas.

The code and output is below.

```html
<html>
<head>
<title>Keyboard input</title>
</head>
<body>
<canvas id="canvas" width="400" height="400" style="border:1px solid #000000;"></canvas>
<script src="https://code.jquery.com/jquery-2.1.0.js"></script>
<script>
var canvas = document.getElementById("canvas");
var cx = canvas.getContext("2d");
var w=canvas.width;
var l=canvas.length;
function rightballposition()
{
cx.clearRect(0, 0, 400, 400);
cx.beginPath();
cx.arc(390, 10, 10, 0, Math.PI * 2);
cx.fill();
}
function leftballposition()
{
cx.clearRect(0, 0, 400, 400);
cx.beginPath();
cx.arc(10, 10, 10, 0, Math.PI * 2);
cx.fill();
}
function centerballposition()
{
cx.clearRect(0, 0, 400, 400);
cx.beginPath();
cx.arc(200, 200, 10, 0, Math.PI * 2);
cx.fill();
}
function downballposition()
{
cx.clearRect(0, 0, 400, 400);
cx.beginPath();
cx.arc(390, 390, 10, 0, Math.PI * 2);
cx.fill();
}
```

```
function downleftballposition()
{
cx.clearRect(0, 0, 400, 400);
cx.beginPath();
cx.arc(10, 390, 10, 0, Math.PI * 2);
cx.fill();
}
var keyc = {
 16: "shift",
 27: "escape",
 32: "space",
 37: "left",
 38: "up",
 39: "right",
 40: "down",
 46: "delete"
};
$("body").keydown(press);
function press(event)
{
if (keyc[event.keyCode]=="right")
{
rightballposition();
}
if (keyc[event.keyCode]=="left")
{
leftballposition();
}
if (keyc[event.keyCode]=="space")
{
centerballposition();
}
if (keyc[event.keyCode]=="down")
{
downballposition();
}
```

```
if (keyc[event.keyCode]=="escape")
{
downleftballposition();
}
}

</script>
</body>
</html>
```

Output:

On pressing right:

On pressing left:

On pressing down:

On pressing space:

On pressing escape:

What does a MouseClick Element Do?

A Mouse element detects the click/motion of the mouse and the location of the mouse cursor on the html canvas when the event happens. It can also perform a certain function when this happens.

MouseClick Example

In the below example, the user checks if the mouse has been clicked on the canvas. It checks for the click using the line:

$("#canvas").click(mousec)

canvas is the name of the html canvas and **mousec** is the name of the function that runs on clicking the mouse. Inside the function, the user writes that the mouse has been clicked.

```
<html>
<head>
  <title>Keyboard input</title>
</head>
<body>
  <canvas id="canvas" width="400" height="400" style="border:1px solid #000000;"></canvas>
  <script src="https://code.jquery.com/jquery-2.1.0.js"></script>
  <script>
  $("#canvas").click(mousec);
  function mousec(event)
  {
  document.write("You just clicked the mouse on the canvas");
  }
  </script>
</body>
</html>
```

233

Output:

After clicking on the canvas:

You just clicked the mouse on the canvas

MouseClick – Hide and Seek

In the below example, we upload a html image and choose a random position on the image as the location of "Tim" in our hide and seek game.

Now, we click on different positions within the image. The program calculates how far the click is from Tim using Pythagros theorem. You can get the image using the link below, or use your own image.

Hide and Seek Picture Link:

https://drive.google.com/file/d/1gmPI4Z2Rm9iAA9vEBi7LWehe-uNE2UQ4/view?usp=sharing

In the below code, **timx** and **timy** are two random numbers between 0 and 500 that determine the x and y co-ordinates of where Tim is hidden in this picture.

mousec(event) is the function that runs when the mouse is clicked. Inside the function **event.offsetX** gives the x co-ordinate of the click and **event.offsetY**

gives the y-coordinate of the click. **ctr** is a counter that counts the number of clicks and increments by 1 inside the **mousec** function.

The program then uses Pythagros theorem to find the distance between Tim and the mouseclick and prints the distance as an alert.

Once the distance is less than 10 pixels; you found Timmy and the program prints out the number of clicks it took.

```html
<html>
<head>
  <title>Find Tim</title>
</head>
<body>
  <h1>Find Tim</h1>
  <img id="hidenseek" src="hidenseek.jpg" width="400" height="400" style="border:1px solid #000000;"></canvas>
  <script src="https://code.jquery.com/jquery-2.1.0.js"></script>
  <script>

  ctr=0;
  var timx=Math.random()*400;
  var timy=Math.random()*400;

  $("#hidenseek").click(mousec);
  function mousec(event)
  {
  dist=Math.sqrt((event.offsetX-timx)**2+(event.offsetY-timy)**2);
  if (dist<10)
  {
  ctr=ctr+1;
  alert("<strong>Congratulations!! You found Tim after "+ctr+" clicks.</strong>");
  }else
  {
  ctr=ctr+1;
  alert("Distance from Tim is "+Math.round(dist));
  }
  }

  </script>
  </body>
  </html>
```

Output:

Hand Calculations (Dist):

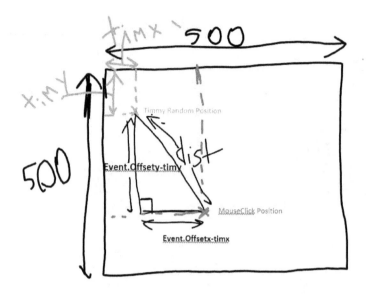

$$Dist = \sqrt{(Event.Offsety - timy)^2 + (Event.Offsetx - timx)^2}$$

MouseClick – Treasure Hunt

The treasure hunt game is very similar to the Hide and Seek Game. There is a different picture, that is the picture of a treasure map. And a random position on the map is the location of the treasure. The program checks for the location of a mouse click and calculates the distance between the clicks and the treasure location. Once the location is within 10 pixels, the treasure is found and the number of clicks taken is printed out.

Treasure Map Link:

https://drive.google.com/file/d/1wPoGYFvwoo2rCJ2eBvA-

9HPAGrAX6v_1/view?usp=sharing

```
<html>
<head>
 <title>Treasure Map</title>
</head>
<body>
 <h1>Find the treasure location</h1>
 <img id="hidenseek" src="treasure-map.jpg" width="400" height="400" style="border:1px solid #000000;"></canvas>
 <script src="https://code.jquery.com/jquery-2.1.0.js"></script>
 <script>

ctr=0;
var jimmyx=Math.random()*400;
var jimmyy=Math.random()*400;

$("#hidenseek").click(mousec);
function mousec(event)
{
dist=Math.sqrt((event.offsetX-jimmyx)**2+(event.offsetY-jimmyy)**2);
if (dist<10)
{
ctr=ctr+1;
alert("<strong>Congratulations!! You found the treasure after "+ctr+" clicks.</strong>");
}else
{
ctr=ctr+1;
alert("Distance from target is "+Math.round(dist));
}
}

</script>
</body>
</html>
```

Output:

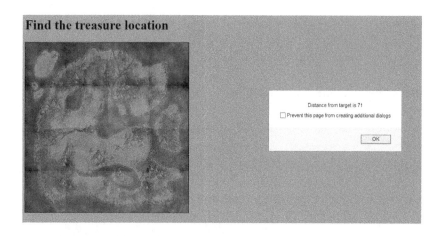

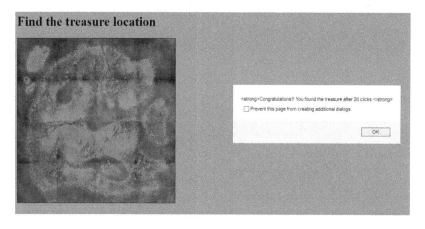

Pong Game

The Pong game is a fun game that builds on the "Bouncing Ball" game on

Page 215 of this book. So, the program has a ball bouncing around the

canvas. We add a bat in the LH corner of the screen that moves up and down.

The bat of length 15 pixels is drawn using **clearRect()** and **fillRect()**. It is set to

a constant xlocation of 10 and the ylocation is defined by a variable called

yrect. yrect is defined in functions **movedown() and moveup()**. Moveup() is

activated when up button is pressed and it decreases yrect by 30 pixels,

which moves the bat up. Movedown() is activated when down button is

pressed and it increases yrect by 30 pixels, which moves the bat down.

Also, the function **press(event)** detects the presence of keys pressed and

activates moveup() and movedown() when up and down button are pressed

respectively.

And we finally have the **frame()** function. It is a function that checks if the ball

is next to the top, bottom and right walls. If the x-coordinate of the ball gets

close to 500, then it is close to the right wall. Then we change the direction of

x-motion to create a bounce back. We do the same thing if the y-coordinate is 0 or 500 (it reaches top/bottom wall), so we change direction of y-motion

for the bounce.

And finally, we have a check to see if the ball touches the bat. We calculate

the distance dist between bat location and ball location using Pythagros

theorem. If the distance (dist) is less than 75 pixels, then we change the

direction of x-motion.

```html
<html>
<head>
  <title>Pong Game</title>
-</head>
<body>
  <canvas id="canvas" width="800" height="600" style="border:1px solid #000000;"></canvas>
  <script src="https://code.jquery.com/jquery-2.1.0.js"></script>
<script>
var canvas = document.getElementById("canvas");
var cx = canvas.getContext("2d");
var w=canvas.width;
var l=canvas.length;
var yrect=0;
cx.beginPath();
cx.clearRect(0, 0, 800, 600);
cx.rect(10, yrect, 15, 90);
cx.fill();
cx.fillStyle = "black";

setInterval(press , 100);


//Ball variables
var snx=1;
var sny=1;
setInterval(frame, 10);
locationx=Math.random()*350;
locationy=Math.random()*350;
```

242

```javascript
function movedown()
{
yrect=yrect+30;
if (yrect>570)
{
yrect=yrect-30;
}
cx.beginPath();
cx.clearRect(0, 0, 800, 600);
cx.rect(10, yrect, 15, 90);
cx.fill();
cx.fillStyle = "black";
}
function moveup()
{
yrect=yrect-30;
if (yrect<0)
{
yrect=yrect+30;
}
cx.beginPath();
cx.clearRect(0, 0, 800, 600);
cx.rect(10, yrect, 15, 90);
cx.fill();
cx.fillStyle = "black";
}

var keyc = {
  16: "shift",
  27: "escape",
  32: "space",
  37: "left",
  38: "up",
  39: "right",
  40: "down",
  46: "delete"
};
$("body").keydown(press);
```

```
function press(event)
{
if (keyc[event.keyCode]=="up")
{
moveup();
}

if (keyc[event.keyCode]=="down")
{
movedown();
}
}
function frame()
{
//Circle
cx.beginPath();
cx.clearRect(20, 0, 800, 600);
cx.arc(locationx,locationy,20,0,2*Math.PI);
cx.fillStyle = "red";
cx.stroke();
cx.fill();
dist=Math.sqrt((locationx-10)**2+(locationy-yrect)**2);
//document.write(dist);
if (locationx>=800)
    {
        snx=snx*-1;
    }
if (dist<75)
    {
        snx=snx*-1;
        locationx=locationx+snx*20;
    }
if (locationy>=600)
    {
        sny=sny*-1;
    }
if (locationy<=0)
    {
        sny=sny*-1;
    }
locationx=locationx+snx*5;
locationy=locationy+sny*5;
}
```

```
</script>
</body>
</html>
```

Output:

Handwritten calculation (distance between bat and ball)

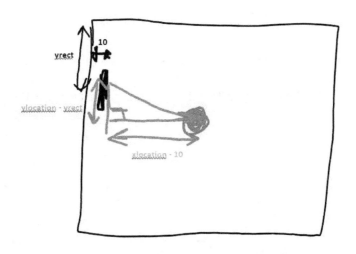

$$Dist = \sqrt{(ylocation - yrect)^2 + (xlocation - 10)^2}$$

1. Write a program that takes in a user input and prints out pictures of 4 animals based on whether the user presses **p,m,a,t** (peacock, monkey, alligator, tiger). For example, if the user presses p, the program shows a picture of a peacock. (Hint: Save the 4 pictures in the same folder. Use the keypress element to detect the presence of the keys, and then the <img> tag to show the pictures).

2. Write a program that shows a simple color chart to the user. The user clicks on one of the colors, and the program prints out the name of the color (Hint: Use the mouseclick to detect the presence and location of the click; and then check if it is close to a particular color).

3. Draw a circle that moves up, down, left and right on the canvas based on whether the user clicks up, down, left and right.

4. To advance on Problem 3, have a treasure placed randomly on the canvas and if the circle gets to within 5 pixels of the treasure, then send a "Congratulations" message.

Conclusion

Thanks for buying the book. I hope you enjoyed it and learnt a lot from the book.

If you were able to go through the exercises in this book by yourself, you are definitely on the right track.

If you'd like any clarification regarding the topics; or any suggestions; please email me at: abiprod.pty.ltd@gmail.com

I also do one-one coaching online if you are interested in personalized help.

If you'd like a more beginner friendly version of this book, you can download my Coding for Kids using JavaScript Book or my Coding for Kids and Beginners using Python.

Other Recommended Books for further reading:

JavaScript: The Good Parts by Douglas Crawford

A Smarter Way to Learn JavaScript

JavaScript: The Definitive Guide

9 781922 462503